Overcome & Succeed with Gratitude

Dr Carolyn Smith-Keune
Helen Cowley
Jodie Eustice
Kathy Shanks
Michele Scott

Nelcia A. Roehm
Patricia Diano
Sharon Le Fort
Taryn Claire Le Nu
Vanessa Cirocco

TurtlePublishing

Copyright © 2022 Turtle Publishing

All rights reserved. No part of this publication may be reproduced, stored in a retrieval system, or transmitted in any form or by any means, electronic, mechanical, photocopying, recording or otherwise, without prior written permission of the author.

Under no circumstances will any blame or legal responsibility be held against the publisher, or author, for any damages, reparation, or monetary loss due to the information contained within this book. Either directly or indirectly. You are responsible for your own choices, actions, and results.

Legal Notice: This book is copyright protected. This book is only for personal use. You cannot amend, distribute, sell, use, quote or paraphrase any part, or the content within this book, without the consent of the author or publisher.

Disclaimer: Please note the information contained within this document is for educational and entertainment purposes only. All effort has been executed to present accurate, up to date, and reliable, complete information. No warranties of any kind are declared or implied. Readers acknowledge that the author is not engaging in the rendering of legal, financial, medical or professional advice. The content within this book has been derived from various sources. Please consult a licensed professional before attempting any techniques outlined in this book.

By reading this document, the reader agrees that under no circumstances is the author responsible for any losses, direct or indirect, which are incurred as a result of the use of the information contained within this document, including, but not limited to — errors, omissions, or inaccuracies.

Published by Turtle Publishing
Cover & Interior Design by Kathy Shanks

turtlepublishing.com.au

Gratitude

Gratitude is being thankful
Finding gems within the dust
It's infectious, like a virus
And spreads like coastal rust

It recalibrates our focus
From the things we can't control
And shifts our eyes from deficit
To the stuff that makes us whole

So I honour those who fill my cup
And I'm thankful every day
For the humans that empower me
With kind things they do and say

I urge us all to see the world
With a perspective that is new
A heart tuned in to gratitude
May enhance your point of view

- Justin Geange

Contents

Nelcia A. Roehm   1
The blessing of gratitude

Sharon Le Fort   17
Can the real Sharon stand up!

Kathy Shanks   37
Overcoming what holds you back

Michele Scott   49
Que sera, sera. Grieving with gratitude.

Vanessa Cirocco   63
Transformation after trauma

Jodie Eustice   77
Be the fabulous You! One's inner self journey

Taryn Claire Le Nu   97
To my beloved gratitude

Patricia Diano   109
Use it or lose it!

Dr Carolyn Smith-Keune   125
Rediscovering gratitude at sea

Helen Cowley   145
Get up and dance.
Your mind is a powerful thing.

Authors   161

INTRODUCTION

It's easy to be grateful when everything is going *right*, isn't it?

You see it all the time. A celebrity bags an award and caps their acceptance speech with a long list of acknowledgments. A pro athlete wins the big game and thanks God, fans, teammates, and others. An old friend gushes appreciatively on social media about how blessed they are with a new baby, a promotion at work, or a family vacation.

That's all well and good—gratitude is a beautiful thing! There's no doubt that these 'highs' must be celebrated with heartfelt thanks.

But, the 'lows' in life can (and do) come. What about then?

It can be extremely tough to find it in yourself to be grateful when you're at the bottom. When obstacles loom so large that they cast dark shadows on everything around you, it can be difficult to see the light of gratitude.

And, the thing is, *that's when it matters the most*.

Science shows that expressing thanks is a natural antidepressant, boosting feel-good chemicals serotonin and dopamine. Gratitude practically equates to happiness, and when else would you need that more than when you're at your lowest? Happiness gives you the strength to persevere and stay resilient as you weather the storm.

In the midst of what can sometimes feel like chaos, gratitude provides a positive focus. It allows you to root in the good as you channel your time, energy, and effort towards your true purpose—your 'why.'

When the road ahead seems endless, gratitude can be powerful fuel for the journey. It enables you to recognise how far you've already come and celebrate exactly where you're at instead of fixating solely on how far you have yet to go.

Gratitude is motivating. It is energising. It is empowering. It can even be life-changing—for the women in this book, that's precisely what it was.

In this book, ten amazing women share their inspiring stories of conquering life's battles. The common thread that runs through them? Facing each twist and turn and navigating through it armed with an incredible spirit of *true* gratitude.

One important thing to recognise is that these women were all *intentional* in cultivating this spirit. After all, gratitude goes far beyond emotion—it is a skill. It's not something that simply comes to you, but a practice to be worked on continuously.

You'll find in this book that one of the most effective ways to practise gratitude is through keeping a written account. Journaling creates a safe, sacred space for processing things and making sense of the world through a lens of mindful positivity.

For each of the authors in this book, gratitude journaling played a crucial role in overcoming the challenges they were dealt with and emerging on the other side all the better for it. Now, not only are they opening up about their experiences, but they are also sharing the valuable tools they've learned along the way.

Just like each person's unique individual story, journaling is a deeply personal experience. If a certain story (or stories!) resonates with you, do consider picking up a copy of the corresponding guided journal. Get in touch with the author directly to find out how—all contact details can be found in their bios at the back of this volume.

So, take a page out of these women's stories—invite gratitude to flow through your journey and watch your own brilliant story unfold.

Chapter 1

Nelcia A. Roehm

The blessing of gratitude

Gratitude is a game changer. It can radically transform your life.

It all started a few months before my twenty-third birthday, when I gave birth to my first son. There was a mixture of excitement and fear for the future, for obvious reasons, but I was mostly excited about becoming a mom. My dreams of parenthood would finally materialize.

I was living the dream! Exactly three months and four days after turning twenty-four, I gave birth to my second son. There was a little less excitement and a lot more fear. Little did I know my stint of motherhood would be the catalyst to transport me into the world of gratitude and its importance for a healthy, balanced life. But it was not always that way.

As far back as I can remember, gratitude was a foreign concept in my life. Sure, I'd heard the word, saw it in print, knew what it meant, but there was no expression of it in my life or in the lives of people around me. I was taught to demonstrate traditional mannerisms, such as saying, "Thank you," and "I appreciate this," when someone gave me something or did something for me. Appreciation was modeled and expected. Good manners were taught and encouraged. After all, it was the norm of the society I grew up in. However, that deep sense of gratitude associated with emotional and mental health benefits that can radically transform your life was non-existent. Gratitude had never been discussed, taught, or encouraged in my childhood or youthful years.

I never had any gratitude role models. I was never told to have gratitude and was totally oblivious to the idea that having gratitude could make a difference in a person's overall wellness. In fact, during the premature days of my life, I was never truly grateful for anything.

On the contrary, if anything, I was ungrateful and focused more on my half empty cup than my blessings, which were truly overflowing.

I didn't see life as a blessing; instead, I viewed my life from the lens of deprivation. I remember as a child I used to covet everything my friends had or did, from their fancy shoes and clothes to the latest toys and gadgets I could never afford. I would often think to myself, *I wish I had one of those*, which led to me feeling inadequate.

It never crossed my mind that even though I didn't have the fancy shoes, clothes, or the gadgets my friends had, I still had a lot to be grateful for. I should have been grateful for the many miracles I experienced daily. For waking up each morning, being able to witness a beautiful sunrise and sunset. I forgot to be grateful for food, clothing, and a place to call home, having all five of my senses, being able to go to school, having a job, and the people who cared about me. I thought it was my right and privilege, not something to be grateful for.

Instead, I grew up always wanting more; more material possessions, especially things I did not and could not have. I felt so deprived by my lack of *stuff* that I believed I was generationally cursed with poverty. I was jealous of everyone who had what I so desperately desired: a beautiful home, a car, nice clothes and shoes – things I thought made life meaningful and gave it beauty. The thought of not having enough always made me sad, and as a result, led to feelings of insecurity, insignificance, inadequacy, and so much unhappiness.

During my high school years, decades ago, there was a popular backpack called a JanSport. It was the thing to have, and if you didn't you were basically a loser. Because of the popularity and high demand of this merchandise, it was very expensive. My caregivers could not afford it. No matter how much I bargained, begged, or pleaded, I was not going to own one of these, which meant I would not be allowed to run with the crowd and fit in with the popular kids. It was the beginning of my sad, unfulfilled life. While I had a backpack to carry my books and supplies, not having that particular brand left a gaping hole in my life that would never be filled.

I spent the first forty years of my life without feeling or experiencing the true meaning of gratitude. But one day something happened that changed the trajectory of my life and greatly impacted my gratitude attitude. Gratitude became real to me when I experienced one of the greatest crises of my adult life.

It was December 2, 2017, a quiet Saturday morning. The sun was doing its best to peek through the clouds, fighting the odds of what was predicted to be a gray and cloudy day, keeping the temperature a little above freezing. *It's going to be a good day*, I thought, as I rolled myself out of bed. I did my morning devotions and immediately began preparing for church. Nothing felt unusual or different that day. In fact, I was very excited because our prospective new pastor was scheduled to speak, and I looked forward to meeting him.

I quickly made my way to the kitchen with a spring in my step and joy in my heart to start making a healthy breakfast. I had barely opened the door of the refrigerator when our home phone rang. My first thought was, it must be one of those telemarketers again, trying to sell me something. I honestly considered not answering for that reason, but also because it was the Sabbath, the day when I shut out the world and focused on spirituality. However, I walked away from my breakfast preparation to the living room, picked up the phone, and said, "Hello."

The voice on the other end of the line said, "Hi, are you Nelcia Roehm?"

I replied, "Yes, I am."

The follow up question was, "Do you have a son?"

At that moment, my heart began pounding and a feeling of fear came over me. Judging from her soft, sympathetic tone, I could sense that something was wrong. I didn't know if it was a mother's intuition or just my uncanny ability to think about the worst-case scenario, but I had a feeling that something terrible had happened.

The voice on the other end explained that she was a chaplain from a local hospital, and she wanted to be sure that she was speaking to the right person – something about HIPAA.

She asked again, "Do you have a son?"

The moment she repeated son, I knew something happened to one of my boys. I didn't know which one, but I began breathing heavily, my heart rate increasing with every second. I could feel my chest pounding. I began to feel weak in my knees, and my whole body grew numb. My heart began to break. I could not contain myself. My husband, who was now in the living room listening to the conversation, witnessing my almost nervous breakdown, wanted to know what was wrong. I handed him the phone because I could no longer contain myself or listen to what she was about to tell me, as if not hearing it would keep it from being real. I let my husband continue the conversation and walked down the hall in what felt like slow motion to my youngest son's room.

With eyes closed, I slowly opened the door, hoping as I opened my eyes, I would see him lying in his bed safe and sound, but instead, his bed was empty, and it looked like it had not been slept in. My heart sank, and the tears came rolling like a dam that had just been breached. I looked out the window; his car was not in the driveway. That was when I knew something had happened to my youngest son, Nertyrus.

By this time, my greatest fears had been confirmed; my husband had received the news that I didn't want to hear. Our twenty-two-year-old son had been involved in a terrible car accident during the early hours of the morning and was in critical condition at the hospital. We were asked to come quickly!

As we made that dreadful drive to the hospital, in that moment of quiet and disbelief, I began to remember all I read and heard about how to face a crisis. I started with prayer. I had no eloquent words or fancy articulations, but in my ramblings between sobs, I simply asked God to save my son's life.

It was a two-year journey of healing and recovery, but God saved my son's life. My prayers were answered, and He gave my son a second chance. That experience, that one life-changing, life-altering experience did the trick. This is when my journey of gratitude began to take shape.

I was thankful for so much in that moment, like my son's life and the fact that there was no one else involved in this crash. There were no other cars; only his. It would have been much worse if other vehicles were involved - we were told, and if there had been anyone in the passenger seat, they would have been crushed to death. According to the police and paramedics, my son should have been dead, but he was alive.

It is said that everything happens for a reason. That is something I never gave much thought to until now. Looking back on this experience, five years later, I now know one of the reasons I encountered this was to learn to truly express gratitude.

Even though my son's accident posed numerous challenges for us, we felt a deep sense of gratitude for all the good things that happened. We received an overwhelming amount of support in every way possible. My son got the best medical care – which we could not afford – and had every bill paid. I was able to both work and take care of his healing and recovery at the same time, and while life was interrupted in many ways, we managed these changes with relative ease and comfort.

I was incredibly grateful!

Behind this dark cloud of life, I saw the silver lining. I saw the blessings. I saw not what we lost, but what we gained, and I was grateful. Something I had failed to express previously in my life had suddenly become the cornerstone of my very existence, my anchor, and now my default attitude!

Somehow through this ordeal, these blessings remained front and center, and I saw everything from that perspective. I felt the utmost gratitude; and suddenly we were able to see our way through the dark cloud. That was a radical shift from what I was used to. This was where my journey of wellness with gratitude at the helm began to take flight.

One-year post-injury, after going through rehab and recovery with my son, I finally felt the weight of the world lift off my shoulders. I was on Christmas break from school, sitting in my office one early morning, reflecting on the year – the struggles, the growth, the wins, the losses. The sun had just come up, and the rays were peering through the window, falling gently on my face, bathing my upper body with warmth as I sank into my comfy chair, enjoying the sweet caress and moment of pure serenity.

I had this powerful thought, sort of like an epiphany, that I should write a book. At first, I was not very clear on what I needed to write and the purpose it would serve; however, I obeyed the prompting, and eventually that thought came to reality in the form of a wellness book for teachers: *Living Your Best Teacher Life*. This book is an expression of the gratitude I felt for how tragedy, struggle, and pain can be used to create strength, determination, and inspiration. This journal is a companion to that book.

One of the greatest benefits of gratitude is the ability to see the silver lining behind every dark cloud. There have been many dark clouds in my life; however, I have handled many of them with grace and perseverance because I have chosen to express gratitude instead of fear.

It is said that gratitude is usually demonstrated when something good happens. When we receive a gift. When life is at its best, not at its worst. However, I have found that when I am grateful, even in the most difficult times, and find at least one thing to be grateful for, I have become more resilient, less depressed, and so much less stressed. So instead of feeling despondent and overwhelmed by life's struggles, I decided to change the narrative. Instead of complaining, or expressing disappointment to others, I create space for the expression of gratitude through journaling. I took up the habit of journaling weekly, not just to record the events of my life for future purposes, but a way to gain clarity and perspective in the moment. I found that putting my thoughts down on paper allowed me to gain a deeper perspective, to find the beauty in my brokenness, and strength in my struggle.

I also kept something called a *God Box*. Instead of worrying or being afraid about what might happen, I wrote my prayers, concerns, and thoughts about whatever situation I was experiencing down on small note cards, and then put them in the box. That way I gave it to God and no longer worried about it. Instead, I gave thanks for whatever outcome I would eventually experience. That helped to literally take my mind off whatever consumed me and focus on what was going right in my life, letting God take care of what was going wrong. That is the blessing of gratitude.

A few summers ago, my husband and I decided to go on vacation to my home island, Saint Lucia, to celebrate our wedding anniversary. We wasted no time planning for this greatly anticipated vacation. We renewed our passports, and we confirmed they'd arrive in time for the trip. We searched for flights, bought tickets, made reservations, and secured accommodations. We got the whole package. My husband and I were so excited to go back to the place where we first met, exchanged our vows, and started our life together. We couldn't wait to see all our friends and connect with people we missed all these years.

Our passports arrived several weeks before our departure. I grabbed the package from the stack of mail in the box and opened the envelope like a kid opens presents on Christmas morning. I was all smiles as I saw all was well with my passport. It was my first American passport, and to say I was excited is an understatement. I then noticed my husband did not have a new passport. Instead, there was a letter with his old passport. My smile quickly faded.

"Honey, we have a problem!" I yelled as I walked toward him with the letter in hand, waving it at him. "You got a letter, and no new passport."

I handed him the letter and waited for him to read it to tell me all would be well. Instead, as he opened the folded note and read silently, I could tell by the cold expression on his face that something was wrong. It turns out that my husband encountered some passport issues that could not be resolved, at least not before our travel date. This meant that our trip to Saint Lucia would need to be put on hold. We tried everything, called everyone we thought could help resolve the issue, but nothing worked out.

"It just wasn't meant to be," I said to myself after I exhausted all my resources. Talk about a big disappointment, but during all this, I couldn't help but feel calm and grateful.

Why, you ask? What did I have to be grateful for when my vacation plans went awry? Simply because I was happy we found this out early enough to create a plan B. As I looked back on the events leading up to this, I felt like the universe was moving us in a better direction. The airlines worked with us, and we were able to keep our same travel dates but go to a different destination. We ended up going to Miami and had the time of our lives.

Even if we didn't get to pursue our original plan, we felt like Miami was where we needed to be. We had some incredible experiences there that we would not have had in Saint Lucia, including knowing how much we would love Florida and one day make it our home.

I truly believe everything always works out for our good. Even when challenges, disappointments, and discontent may come our way, there is something good in there when we take the time to dig a little deeper and find it. Expressing gratitude for everything transports you into a whole new mindset. You gain a higher perspective. You begin to see the glass as half full instead of half empty. You begin to act differently. Suddenly, life looks better from where you're standing.

Today, gratitude has led me to experience a satisfaction that is beyond material achievement, beyond having everything go my way. It's a deep sense of fulfillment that comes from knowing everything happens for a reason, and the result, no matter how bad the situation is or how long it takes, is always good.

Gratitude is an intentional action. We must decide to feel it, harness it, grow it, and experience it fully. It is not a magic pill for curing all of life's difficulties, but it is pretty magical in reframing our perspectives on life's let-downs. When gratitude comes in, anxiety walks out. The best way to deal with stress, anxiety, and disappointment is to demonstrate gratitude repeatedly. It means counting your blessings, not your losses, to see the good and focus on what's right instead of what's wrong. Knowing you already have everything you need in you and the outward blessings are just a manifestation of that belief.

Gratitude is indeed a game changer!

You can create this in your own life in a few simple ways. First, you must intentionally decide to practice gratitude daily. It's as simple as waking up in the morning, looking in the mirror, and saying:

I am so grateful to be alive!

I woke up this morning!

I am so excited for another day!

Today is going to be a great day!

It's your experience, you choose your language. It's all about having the presence of mind to know and understand there is another possible scenario where you didn't wake up — but you did. Be mindful of that. That should be enough to spark life and energy and to set your vibration high. That should be enough to change your mindset, to change the narrative of your day, and to set you up for success every day.

But here's the most powerful thing you can do: create the gratitude effect through journaling. Taking time daily, weekly, or monthly, whichever works for you, to record events of your life is a great tool you can use to create a life of gratitude. Being intentional about expressing gratitude, recognizing it, and creating it, can be an amazing way to increase your gratitude meter.

You have heard me share how gratitude has dramatically changed my life. How just being grateful and mindful has helped me through some of the most difficult seasons. I want you to experience that, too. I dare you to take this challenge. Thirty days of gratitude to living your best life. Every day, you will have something to do, an action to take, that will increase your attitude of gratitude. So come on, grab your pen, and let's get started on living your best life through gratitude!

Chapter 2

Sharon Le Fort

Can the real Sharon stand up!

With a freshly made coffee, it was the perfect time to come outside in the warmth of the sun and start writing. Along with my laptop and notebook, I brought out my youngest son's speaker to listen to some tunes, as I got in the mood to take a dive into my thoughts and share my story with you all, including how gratitude showed up in my life.

Guess what happened?

The sun disappeared, the clouds came over, and next thing 'Cold as Ice' by Foreigner came over the speaker.

How's that for you... What a way to start this project off.

It's the fourth time I have co-authored an anthology, sharing my truth of my past and how I transformed my life throughout the chaos.

As usual, it's not until I sit down and start typing that the words come together. Right up to the moment of fingers on the keypad, ready to type; I've no idea what is going to be shared with you.

Please nurture yourself along the way as you read my journey.

Some might wonder what music I'm listening to, right now?

"It's Urgent," by Foreigner.

It doesn't take me long to go back to that period of time, the 1980s. The 80s could be described as not only the worst but also the best time for me.

I was 14, and up to then, I lived in what could be described as a battle zone fraught with domestic and family violence and sexual abuse. Growing up surrounded by life-threatening violence and subjected to covert sexual abuse, I not only witnessed but also experienced countless instances of perverse cruelty and mistreatment. It was these traumatic events that would lead me into my own private war.

As previously described in my chapter within Emma Hamlin's 'Change Makers' series, "Living in a perpetual cycle of terror had a significant impact on my life, feelings of unworthiness, fight-or-flight reactions, people-pleasing, difficulty with emotional regulation, sex and alcohol, comfort eating or should I say, 'emotional bingeing' and most of all I never felt like I belonged."

Since I wrote those words, I've gone farther in my healing journey to uncover the depths of the impact of all I witnessed and experienced.

Living that life was the reason I can resonate with tv shows and movies based on black ops and cover ups. It's the underlying deep secret that causes the most impact that we bear witness to.

We spend our time viewing behaviour rather than uncovering the inherent cause of it, and for years unknowingly living in what is known as 'survival' mode. Surviving is exactly what we have to do to keep alive. To keep ahead of what's seen as a threat.

I'm going to share with you something I've only shared with a few people up till now, the true impact long-term, frightening childhood trauma had on my life.

I'm now in a place of my healing that I'm ready to publicly discuss it.

You may have questions afterwards, and that's okay; I will try to explain it as much as I can within this space. I also plan to continue to share this information, to bring awareness of the potential impacts from a lived experience.

I had been diagnosed with Dissociative Identity Disorder. You may be thinking right now, what does this even mean?

As stated on the Mayo Clinic website, "Dissociative disorders usually develop as a way to cope with trauma. The disorders most often form in children subjected to long-term physical, sexual or emotional abuse or, less often, a home environment that's frightening or highly unpredictable. The stress of war or natural disasters also can bring on dissociative disorders."[1] In my situation, I witnessed extremely frightening violent abuse in conjunction with sexual and emotional abuse. As a result, alters were created throughout my

---

1 https://www.mayoclinic.org/diseases-conditions/dissociative-disorders/symptoms-causes/syc-20355215#:~:text=Dissociative%20 disorders%20are%20mental%20disorders,with%20functioning%20 in%20everyday%20life.

childhood to protect me from the experience, and although it's still something I'm processing, I also am on the journey of getting to know each part of 'ourselves.'

Before I go further into 'our' story, you might get a bit confused with pronouns... when there is an 'I,' that is me (Sharon), 'Our' is all parts of us (alters), and Shazz (one of my alters).

By my mid-to late teens, I had been 'groomed' enough to be seen as 'prey' for others' pleasures; at 14 I was raped, as well as being subjected to covert sexualised behaviours by individuals who were adults (the ones I was meant to trust).

At 18, I left one war zone and moved onto another. This time, it was with alcohol and sex. There is dangerous line between 'exciting' and 'reckless.'

For me, in my situation, we viewed sex as something that you are meant to do; if you don't do what is expected, then there will be devastating consequences. Although I was not living within that war zone any longer, the impact of the life I had prior was firmly imprinted, and therefore, the warrior within turned the tables around and became the seeker.

I'm going to introduce you to Shazz – my warrior (alter).

If it weren't for Shazz, I wouldn't be here as I am today!

I've come to a point of acceptance and understanding of these moments where Shazz stood strong and took no crap from others, and didn't say no to propositions of group sex, kink, and binge drinking. She said – 'Bring it.'

Shazz presents when I'm not strong enough for the situation at hand. She's the 'protector'!

For instance, at 18, leaving my war zone and going into a similar territory of men and drinking, I had no idea how to behave, let alone feel like I had anything intelligent enough to say to hold a conversation.

Shazz knew how to manage that – she joined them.

She drank, danced, and flirted; there was no pulling punches and wondering what the night was going to look like.

It just happened!

Shazz has her own persona; she walks with an air of absolute confidence; she will make direct eye contact with men who think they are being covert. She loves to drink…At 18 it was cocktails such as screaming orgasms, quick fucks, anything with multiple amounts of alcohol to bring the best of her 'out,' loud music to dance to; in the 80s it was Billy Idol, The

Radiators, and anything else like it. She will swear, like a trooper, because she can.

She is, as a friend of mine named her fittingly, 'Shazza Fierce.'

Shazz loves all things risqué, pushing those boundaries just a bit further each time.

Through therapy, I've connected; Shazz has been with me since at least my early teens, even earlier. There is one instance, at 15, I stood in front of three burly men and told them to either help my mother from being killed or get the fuck back in their house.

Not long after, I told the person who was beating the hell out of my mother that if they came near me, we would call the police and charge their arse!

I always wondered where I got the courage to speak like that.

That particular time was the first time I experienced non-fatal strangulation!

How did I/we survive? Shazz – that's how.

She has an incredible inner warrior strength and a way of seeing exactly what's in front of her and will deal with it head on. Now, this was great when we needed to 'survive,' but in all honesty, it wasn't great in everyday life.

I would go from kind and compassionate to feisty and angry, like we were ready to go into battle.

When there was a perceived threat, Shazz would come in, and before I knew it, it was different. I would feel something had changed but had no idea in what way.

I would go from 'nice girl' to completely unfiltered. Think jeans, boots, leather jacket, with a look of 'I dare ya to fuck with me.'

Fast forward to my mid-thirties – I was now divorced after a 14-year marriage to someone I had put on a pedestal for too many years. I followed him up and down the east coast of Australia while he figured out his career.

Throughout those years, Shazz appeared frequently. The ex-husband was always saying we were 'just like your family,' that 'I was too fat,' 'not thin/pretty/smart enough.' Shazz would appear, constantly yelling, 'I'm not fucken who you say I am' or 'stop fucking talking to me like that.'

Shazz would take it further and call him a fucken arsehole, or to shut the fuck up.

I had stopped drinking years before our divorce as I took motherhood very seriously and was very nurturing and affectionate with my young children.

However, that changed after divorce.

Our son was 9 at the time of our separation and eventually moved to the other parent's place at 11. I was utterly devasted.

There are no words to aptly describe the pain I felt that day as my beautiful boy, my first born, drove away in his other parent's car. It felt like my entire world just buckled, and I had no strength to continue. I knew I had my daughter to care for, but the pain was deeply raw. It was like the other parent had come into my life and took the very thing that meant the world to me, ripped it from my arms along with the invisible umbilical cord, between us.

I couldn't imagine a life without my son. He slowly disappeared from not only my life but also his sister's.

The most extremely horrendous grief remained buried deep within, for years. Not being able to watch my brave, beautiful son grow up and have the childhood he so deserved. The pain was unbearable!

Every time that pain would seep to the surface, Shazz appeared. The tone of my voice would change, and I would start snapping at people; my frustration at the world or the situation would be completely overwhelming, and at times Shazz would just say exactly what I was afraid of saying.

Shazz took over for a while; we shifted in and out. I needed her strength to fight through the pain. By this time, we were fully in 'survival' mode.

Then along came the *first* turning point...

I was sitting out the back of the house, on a day much like today. Where I was living with my daughter, at the time, feeling the desperation of needing to bring income into our house. I considered becoming a sex worker. I thought, if I was expected to be this person, I should be earning money from it.

I sat, phone in hand, looking at an advertisement I'd seen in the paper. But as I reached to dial, a small voice inside me became louder and louder saying, "This is not you!"

Up until recently, I always thought it was my 'intuition' or 'gut instinct' kicking in, but it was in fact another part of me, making themselves known to me.

After what felt like the longest 30 seconds, I put the phone down, got out a journal and pen, and asked myself brutally honest questions:

- What the fuck do you want in your life?
- How are you going to make it happen?
- When are you going to do it?

Keep in mind, I had Shazz in the background; she loved to have her input.

I then wrote out my five-year plan.

What I listed at that time was:

- Gain a qualification in youth work and work with young people
- $5,000 in the bank
- Purchase a car
- Have both my children in my life

It doesn't seem like a lot, but when you're living on government allowances and fending off breach notices for not paying rent on time, it was huge!

I went on to break it down into actionable steps....

I was able to set forth and locate an online course and enrol into the Certificate IV Youth Work.

I found a local youth drop-in centre to volunteer and gain skills in working with young people.

I would love to say it all fell into place, and everything was absolutely fantastic, and we lived happy ever after... Sadly, life doesn't work like that.

At the very same time, I was also experiencing emotional and financial abuse from my ex-husband and couldn't continue full-time study. I had to let it go for a while, as I desperately needed to get back to work. I saw this not as failure, just taking a bit of detour to achieve my goals. I found myself working in a part-time data entry role, aiming to be there for my daughter, and started working on my savings plan to keep the 'wolves' from the door.

Life continued as is, at least for a while. I was continually going in and out of 'survival' mode. Shazz appeared mostly towards the end of the week, making plans to go out.

At this time in my life, I had no idea that I was disassociating and thought this was just me being me and doing what I did 'best.' Shazz was the one who loved to turn the music up and get wasted, before even stepping out of the door. Meet random guys who could provide some 'fun.'

One of these nights, I met a guy…or, I should say, Shazz met him.

About 12 months later, he had begun calling me more. A quick chat here and there. One day he asked me out to dinner. Now remember, he met Shazz, who is wild, crazy, and gets drunk.

Me, I love meaningful conversations and having a laugh. There was hardly any conversation; as I learnt over time, he wasn't a big conversationalist, unless it was football or some other kind of sport. There was, however, this energy that was very captivating; he had this 'bad-boy' air about him. All I kept thinking was, what is it that has me coming back for more?

Four months after we officially became a 'couple,' we found out I was pregnant. Both of us were in our early forties, with children from previous marriages. About 18 months later, as a full-time stay-at-home mum with a toddler, I pondered the question – what's next for me?

I remembered the goals I'd written down a few years prior. I called TAFE about my prior studies. I could re-enrol into the course and get credits for the work already completed. YAY!

I kept bumping into a friend of mine, each time speaking about doing a placement where she was the coordinator of housing program in a community organisation.

Within 12 months of that decision, I had been gainfully employed one day a week within a youth housing program, had almost finished my course, and had already completed several units for a social housing qualification. Within two years, I had moved into another youth housing program and successfully completed a diploma of community services and a qualification in mental health.

Yet, there was something missing.

My application to be a brokerage administrator was successful. I was now responsible for approving grants for young people transitioning into independent living.

Enormous moment for me... I also had been offered a spot at university, to complete the Bachelor of Counselling.

I loved my job, my kids were growing up, my eldest was back in my life, and then...

A change of management happened at work; this person was not as experienced as my prior manager. Covert narcissist behaviours occurred, and I felt my body reacting in ways I had not experienced in years.

My hands would shake as I went back to my office from his. I'd sit at my desk, tears streaming down my face. My flight/fight/freeze reactions kicking in fast.

Shazz emerged!

I would shut down conversations and call out his behaviours. It was happening without me being consciously aware. After being told by the head manager I was the problem, I found my voice and said, "Sorry, I disagree with this."

I resigned the following week, and shortly after leaving my job. I had my breakdown/breakthrough.

Second turning point...

One of the biggest gifts came into my life, and that is my/our therapist, Juliana.

I knew I was safe with Juliana. The very first appointment she said, "I'm here for the long haul." It's been five years now.

Eight months into therapy, I connected – I was, in fact, a survivor! I never had seen myself as a 'survivor' until this moment in time. What a lightbulb moment that was!

It was also when I understood all the sexualised behaviours I had witnessed and experienced as a child and adolescent were in fact sexual abuse/assault.

It was not normal to have been around this kind of environment.

This insight gave me the clarity to understand that what I had been experiencing during sex was, in fact, dissociation! I began to comprehend how there are alternate parts of me that have their own unique priorities and needs as well as distinct ways of expressing themselves.

Juliana encouraged me to journal as much as I could. To nurture and be really kind to myself in the process.

Although, I had been journalling on and off for years. I did exactly as Juliana had encouraged. I journalled. I found myself writing verses about the pain, allowing it to pour out on the pages, tears flowing... as well as writing three things I was grateful for each day, no matter how small.

I find journalling very cathartic, where I can write my thoughts and feelings without reason or judgement.

I'm profoundly grateful for everything that had led me to exactly where I am right at this moment.

Sounds weird, right?

Sitting here, sharing this incredible journey with you, reflecting on the multi-layered horrific abuse I experienced throughout most of my life, I'm so bloody grateful for the team of protectors I had on my side, ensuring I was safe, keeping me moving forward.

I've carried so much shame from the experiences and activities I found myself participating in. Not realising that they were maladaptive behaviours. Now, that shame has been released; it has been replaced with gratitude and love for all parts of me, especially Shazz, as she kept me alive!

It takes an enormous amount of energy most days to keep all parts of us 'happy.'

So now, I embrace Shazz's taste in music and play her genre of music in the car a couple of times of week. I also wear jeans and boots to work at least once a week, but I make sure I have the choice of jacket (we can't turn up to work in leather).

Now it's my turn to guide Shazz to less destructive ways of embracing our uniqueness, and one of the ways we are learning to communicate is through the practice of journalling, especially with me expressing my gratitude for each of my alters and how they have helped me to navigate life.

Shazz and a couple of other alters find journalling boring, so my journalling practice varies; I go from free writing to a more practical way to create a plan of attack (the Shazz influence).

We need the WHY and WHAT?

- What do we want in our life?
- Why do we want this?
- What is it going to bring to our life?
- Why is that important to us?

There is no right or wrong way of journalling. However, to get the most out of journalling, I've found you must:

- **Surrender**...all limitations and perceived expectations that you have of yourself and be open to your inner voice and the wisdom shared from within.

- **Acknowledge**...your dreams, your past, your desires.

- **Reflect on**...the balance in your life, your intentions, and defining your goals.

Becoming more aligned with yourself, you will create a life that is more than balanced and aligned with what/who you are here to do/be.

Seeing our time together is ending, for now, I want to share a couple of our biggest achievements.

As a kid who dropped out of school at 14.

I've gone on to be a multi-time Amazon international best-selling co-author, to working behind the scenes on the education and research committee of a Brisbane-based domestic and family violence charity.

Co-creating programs for survivors to rebuild their lives, as well as becoming a speaker on the impact of childhood domestic violence and sexual abuse.

I also courageously launched my coaching business, *Sharon Le Fort -Speaker Author Coach*. Empowering women to recognise their strengths, to gain confidence and belief that anything is possible; and I will continue to share the message of **'Stand strong in your truth as it's your truth and no one can take that from you!'**

Our truth is...

I'm Sharon Le Fort, and my mission is to guide and facilitate the healing of those who are forgotten survivors of childhood domestic and family abuse, and de-stigmatize the impact of childhood domestic and family abuse, mental health and dissociative identity disorder.

Chapter 3

Kathy Shanks

Overcoming what holds you back

"Don't walk away from me, you bitch!"

I don't know how long he'd been yelling and criticising on this particular day. I'd finally had enough. I was crying so hard I couldn't see very well, so I left. I walked out the door. Half way across the cul-de-sac, when I was in the middle of the street, he screamed those words at me. Surely all the neighbours heard. I think I might have stopped breathing for a few moments. Thankfully, my legs seemed to keep moving until I was out of sight, through the pathway between the houses across from our home. I couldn't breathe properly and sucked in air between sobs. He'd never called me *that* before. I mean, he'd always been mean. I don't remember a time when he was nice. But he'd never said that word or called me something so awful.

I was 11. That man was the person I believed to be my father.

I grew up thinking I wasn't anything special. It wasn't a bad childhood. We lived in the suburbs in a three-bedroom, one-bath house with a family of four children and two adults. I was the eldest, and I remember my mum working long hours at certain times of the year. During those times, my dad had me do a lot of work around the house, helping out with my younger siblings. I honestly can't even remember the specifics of how I was treated, but I had an overwhelming feeling of being unwanted. I often spent entire weekends at my best friend's house to stay away. I didn't really understand why I was treated so differently to my brother and sisters; I just knew that they could do whatever they wanted, and I would get in to trouble all the time. Even when I thought I was doing the right thing, there was always yelling. I was always in the wrong. I was never good enough.

I distinctly remember trying to fall asleep at night. Most nights I'd be overthinking the events of the day. I often struggled to get to sleep. I'd lie in bed with a million thoughts in my head: "What did I do wrong?", "Why did I get in trouble for that?" I used to soothe myself by imagining that my real father had actually been kidnapped by aliens. I'd play out the whole story, where one day a man would come back and unzip the suit around my father to reveal he was really an imposter pretending to be my father. I might have been watching Scooby-Doo cartoons at the time, because my real father was always hidden underneath a mask. It never occurred to me that my 'real father' would look different, though. And, it really never occurred to me that my imagination was partial truth.

The day he called me a bitch has stayed fixed in my mind, even over 35 years later. I felt like I'd been slapped in the face. After I'd walked through the alley, I stayed out of sight for quite some time, trying to calm down. *What should I do now?* I snuck back to the house after a while to get my bike, and rode all the way to where my mum was working. I'd never ridden that far before. It was such a long way. But I just had to tell someone. *Surely Mum would finally see the truth of this awful man who treated me so badly. Surely she'd see how upset I was. Surely this was the final straw, and something would finally change.*

I rode and rode and rode. Thoughts circulated in my head about what he'd said, how I felt, how I was able to ride so very far. My mum would be just as enraged as I was. My thoughts and feelings would be vindicated. Tears rolled down my face all the way there. *This had to be it, right? Something had to be done.*

I finally arrived at Mum's work. I can't even remember what I finally said to her, but I remember that her response was overwhelmingly underwhelming. Mum barely acknowledged what I said. There was no outrage like I thought there would be. There were no repercussions for his behaviour. It was just, 'Oh, that's no good. Let's go home and sort out dinner.' Ummmm, what??

As an adult looking back, I know my emotions were escalated. And I know my mother acknowledged my distress more than I remember. But I felt so deflated that she didn't acknowledge what had happened to the extent that I was expecting. My 11-year-old brain just heard, 'I'm not important enough for this to make a difference.'

And that's the mindset I held on to for many years.

'I'm not important'.

When my dad was nicer to my siblings – *I'm not important*. When I didn't get invited to a party – *I'm not important*. When a friend had to cancel on me – *I'm not important*. When someone didn't offer to help me – *I'm not important*.

It's this self-limiting belief that held me back from reaching my true potential for many years.

Less than a year after that particular incident, we were staying at my grandparents' house. It was my favourite time of the year, when all my aunts and uncles travelled to Queensland for Christmas. After the usual Christmas events, Mum and Dad flew back to Sydney, leaving me and my siblings with my grandparents. A few days later, Mum showed back up at Nanny's house. She had the car full of things from our house, and our little puppy dog, Sandy. As soon as she said we were staying in Queensland, and away from 'him', I literally jumped up and down. I was so incredibly happy. We were moving, and we were moving far away, permanently.

A couple of years after our move, I discovered that that man wasn't actually my biological father. This discovery made me smile for weeks. I finally felt somewhat vindicated that I wasn't imagining my feelings. It all made sense, and the continued separation of his attitude and treatment towards me was less hurtful. Years later, of course, I realised that it really wasn't about me. His behaviour was about him.

As it often does, life went on and I grew up. I went to uni. I began my career. I met and married the love of my life, a man who treats me like I'm important and makes me happy every day. We've had two wonderful children together, and I've started a couple of businesses that allow me to juggle home and work life in the way that I choose. Being a parent is my favourite 'job', and I'm so grateful for every experience this brings to my life. One of the things that makes me feel most grateful is watching the relationship my husband has with our children. It's a beautiful thing to witness unconditional love and to understand the long-term impact this can have for your own children.

I also attended a lot of self-development events and read a lot of books. I discovered gratitude for everything in my life. I found peace in the understanding that everything happens for a reason. I forgave the man I thought was my father for so many years. I began to understand that he did the best that he could. It was a different time, and he had his own childhood challenges to overcome.

It took a lot of years for me to feel my own self-worth. Forgiving my 'father' and removing the hate and hurt from that relationship was the beginning of a happier and calmer life.

This isn't really a story about how I found or lost gratitude. In fact, I didn't even know that 'gratitude' was something you could intentionally do until I was in my thirties. Gratitude kind of crept up, like a sloth, because it really took over 10 years to feel the full power of gratitude. It was a slow burn, but completely worth it.

For me, living in gratitude brings me peace. I usually don't sweat the small stuff that happens in everyday life. The world is full of challenges: difficult people, difficult relationships, price rises, naughty children, money problems, health problems...the list goes on. Sure, you may have to communicate with people who you don't meet eye to eye with, but gratitude can help you to appreciate their role in your life. Sure, you may have someone cut you off in traffic, but gratitude helps you to understand that perhaps that delay saved you from having an accident later. Sure, your refrigerator breaking is a hassle, but perhaps it happened at a time when you didn't lose a fridge full of food. Most things have a silver lining; gratitude can help you not only find it but also use those negatives for something positive.

This story is actually a story about how my childhood defined the way I saw the world. It defined how I reacted to people around me. It defined how I felt about myself. For years, I was told I wasn't important enough. For years, I allowed my perception of what others thought of me to define how I felt about myself. It was gratitude that allowed me to finally overcome these feelings. We all have those deeply ingrained beliefs that hold us back in life. Those beliefs are how we view the world. Practising gratitude has finally allowed me to manage those ingrained beliefs from when I was a child.

What I want to share the most is that despite your upbringing, despite your beliefs, despite the people around you – you can use gratitude to overcome the things that are holding you back. Working on finding gratitude every day can give you a better understanding of yourself.

I'd love to share my most recent discovery. I regularly use my journal to do three things: I express gratitude for what I HAVE in my life, I express gratitude for what I WANT in my life, and I create affirmations that will help me

BRIDGE the gap. I've been doing this for years, and it has had a big impact on my personal and professional goals. Now, from my story, you know that my most dominant limiting belief is that I'm not important enough. When journaling, I regularly express gratitude for success and achievement in my life. My affirmations often include statements like, "I am enough," "I am achieving my goals," "I am kicking goals." I have been actively working towards shifting my mindset away from my limiting belief. For the most part, this works and I manage to keep that feeling away. What I only just realised, to my surprise, is that I've actually been working TOWARDS things that make me feel important. I've subconsciously created opportunities in my life that have given me significance. I was recently invited to become a Director on the Board for the Kids4Kids Foundation. It wasn't until I started doing this that I realised I've been creating opportunities in my life that set me up for success. My minor charitable activities have escalated to a position where I can begin to help make a real impact for disadvantaged children. I've also created work opportunities that allow me to help others become significant in their chosen field, which makes me feel immensely proud. While I didn't actively seek out these roles, I know my journaling and expressions of gratitude have been the driving force behind the current direction of my life. For this, I am immensely grateful!

Finding gratitude was the first step in finding peace. Finding gratitude gave me an appreciation for my relationship with my 'father'. That relationship gave me a lot of things that make me who I am today. Gratitude gave me acceptance. Gratitude gave me the ability to embrace the parts of me that feel broken and channel them into something bigger than myself. You really never lose those deep ingrained feelings that you've developed in these earlier years, but you don't have to let them define you for the rest of your life.

So, how do you practice gratitude? Well, the answer is…however you want to. You can make a note of three things each day that make you happy; you could meditate; you could spend time with people and discuss what you loved about your day; you could journal in a variety of ways. The list is truly endless. The one thing you MUST do is actually 'do it'. When tragedy hits someone you know or love, it's often said, "Go home and hug your babies, love your parents, *carpe diem*, you only live once." Why wait for tragedy to enjoy the good things in life, though? I believe if we live a life in gratitude, we shouldn't have any regrets.

Now, don't get me wrong. I don't live a 'blissful' life of pure gratitude. It's a work in progress every day. The act of practising gratitude with intention is how I do my best to really appreciate and live my life. Finding gratitude is a daily exercise. We must commit to practising it, and act with gratitude daily. I use my journal to remind myself to keep gratitude at the forefront of my mind. Over the years I've had a variety of journaling practices, but one thing has remained constant: I always express gratitude. As a part of this project, I've created a journal for you to focus on finding gratitude, and to use gratitude to manifest what you really want. This process is simple: express gratitude for what you HAVE, express gratitude for what you WANT, and create affirmations to BRIDGE the gap in your skills, actions, and beliefs.

We all have dreams in life, and you can use gratitude to achieve those dreams. If you're constantly feeling like you're going two steps forward and one step back, gratitude may just be the missing piece to your happiness. Expressing gratitude for what you WANT is a form of manifesting, plus it has the added bonus of making us DECIDE what we want. When you know what you want and commit to reminding yourself what it is, you're letting the universe know your intentions.

Bridging the gap with affirmations is how I continue to uplevel my life. I know who I am NOW, but who do I have to become to attain my wildest dreams. What skills do I have to develop? What actions do I need to take? What thoughts are holding me back? What new thoughts do I need to develop to reach my goals?

Once I feel gratitude for what I have, I can express gratitude for the future and then begin to develop the mindset for what I really want.

One of my favourite quotes...

> *Gratitude is not only the greatest of virtues but the parent of all others.*
>
> – Marcus Tullius Cicero

Indeed, gratitude is the beginning of true happiness.

Chapter 4

Michele Scott

Que sera, sera.
Grieving with gratitude.

Growing up, my mum would often sing:

> Que sera, sera,
> Whatever will be, will be,
> The future's not ours to see,
> Que sera, sera.
> What will be, will be.

In the spring of 2004, Mum asked if I could do a Tarot reading for her. For the previous couple of years, she had been hearing about my spiritual studies, primarily in the ancient arts of Tarot and Numerology, and she thought it was time I put my newfound knowledge into practice. I was hesitant. Tarot was not my first love, and I was somewhat wary of its reputation as a fortune-telling tool. I was much more comfortable with the science of Numerology. I found its practical application as a self-development and life improvement tool much more useful in modern days and times. But Mum was excited about receiving a Tarot reading, so I gave her my Rider Waite Tarot Cards and guided her through the shuffling process before laying out the cards using the Celtic Cross spread.

Popular in Tarot, the Celtic Cross spread gives valuable insight into where the individual is at on a physical, mental, and emotional level and also provides insight into past choices, future outcomes, opportunities, hopes, and dreams. What stands out the most about this moment in time with my mum was seeing the Death card show up in the reading. The Death card in Tarot usually refers to endings and phases of completion rather than physical death, but I felt an immediate sense of heaviness and doom. I brushed it aside. I chided myself for being dramatic; to Mum, I remarked that this card could be a healthy and positive sign of turnarounds and new beginnings to come.

The following year was 2005, and from almost the beginning of the year, Mum complained of feeling unwell. It began with experiencing numbness on one side of her mouth; however, after a visit to her doctor, she was reassured and told there was nothing to worry about. I questioned this when I found out about it, much later on, and wondered why this hadn't been seen as a red flag; as Mum was relatively fit, healthy, and rarely ill, at the time it seemed sensible to believe that a virus or some passing infection was the cause. She had given up smoking several years earlier and had never been one to drink alcohol. She was also active and engaged with her grandchildren, teaching, playing, and taking them for bike rides most days and riding her bike along with them.

By this point, I was teaching at the spiritual college I had studied at, and Mum looked after my son when I taught in the evenings. As I'd been a single mum from the onset, my mum had been there from the beginning of my pregnancy and was present in the labour room when I gave birth to my boy. Mum was my right-hand woman; she supported and helped me throughout my early journey as a mum, and if I didn't see her every single day, I spoke to her on the phone instead. She was an integral part of my life.

As the year went by, Mum continued to feel not quite right. She was never bedridden but was certainly unwell and losing weight she didn't need to lose – she was actively trying to put on weight. I urged her to get a second opinion. Repeated visits to her doctor were not providing any answers, and it didn't seem as if her doctor was investigating the matter with any sense of urgency if at all.

"You don't owe your doctor any loyalty, Mum," I said one evening after returning from work, noticing that she had lost more weight and was still complaining of feeling a bit off. It was time to get a second opinion!

By now the word cancer was showing up in my thoughts, but I was naively positive about it. Even when I remembered back to the Death card in the Tarot reading the previous year, I still felt that if the diagnosis were cancer, it would simply be a challenge to overcome and not a death sentence. Despite the terrifying dream I had around this same time.

In the dream scene, I was in a water park, similar to Wet & Wild on the Gold Coast in Queensland. It was manic. There was lots of activity – people climbing upstairs and flying down slides. It seemed like mayhem, and I felt frantic in the dream.

In real life at the time, my son was experiencing difficulties at school; I was navigating and negotiating his time spent with his troubled father, and I was worried about my mum. I had a lot on my mind and a lot going on as well, juggling single motherhood with a new career in the spiritual wellness field.

In the dream, I saw my son at the top of the stairs, about to go down the other side of the slide, and I was terrified that he would be hurt or harm himself. I shouted, "Jaymon, wait for me!" as I pushed through the throngs of people between us, but by the time I powered my way through to the top of the stairs, my son had disappeared. He wasn't anywhere to be seen. Instead, when I reached the top of the stairs, I saw my mum and dad on the other end of the slide, as if they were waiting there to catch my son. This was reassuring for a second or two, and then suddenly I felt myself being locked into a cage of some sort, as if it was my turn to go down the slide.

In the dream, I was taken by surprise, and then, instead of going down the slide, I plunged immediately into the water, still locked in the cage. I panicked. "I am going to drown" was my first coherent thought as water surged around me. Terror seized me – but only until my next thought: "Relax. Just relax. Just breathe". I knew panic would lead to death, so if I just relaxed, let go, and breathed through it, I would be okay.

I have always been a prolific dreamer. I had terrifying nightmares as a child, and until I delved deeper as an adult into dream analysis, my dreams frightened me. I have read many dream interpretation books over the years and researched many different theories of dream analysis. It has been enlightening, to say the least, and helpful to learn about dream types. Water dreams can refer to our emotions, and buildings can show how we construct our lives, whilst flying dreams can give us insight into our mental states, innovation, and elevated thinking.

I woke from the water park dream, immediately feeling that an unexpected emotional journey was heading my way – one that would overwhelm me and make me feel as if I were drowning. Yet the dream was also reassuring, a reminder that if I let go, relaxed, and remembered to breathe, I would be okay.

In the midst of all of this, Mum also commented on another foreboding incident: frequent visits from my Uncle Cecil. He lived a 30-minute drive away, and his usual visiting routine involved popping in every couple of months or so. But Mum said he'd been coming around every couple of weeks, so often and regularly that she'd been provoked into saying, "Cecil, who's dying? You or me?!"

About a month before the end of 2005, Mum woke up with a crook neck. Her neck was stiff and sore, so she paid another visit to the doctor.

This time, though, her usual doctor wasn't available, and she saw a different doctor, who upon hearing about the weight loss said there were only three reasons why people lose weight. One: they are actively trying to lose weight; two: depression; or, three: it's an indicator of cancer. Straight away, this doctor organized for Mum to be tested via an MRI, and quickly after that she was diagnosed with lung cancer.

Chemotherapy treatment happened quickly after this; however, after only a couple of sessions, things took a sudden turn for the worse. I couldn't get through to my parents on this particular day as I headed to work, which was odd, as they had both retired by then and were mostly always home. After work, when I rang again, I learned from Dad that Mum had had a mini-stroke and been admitted to Dandenong Hospital.

I headed to the hospital first thing the next morning. Driving there, I cast my mind back to the year before, remembering Mum complaining about numbness on one side of her mouth, and I wondered if that too had been some sort of stroke that quietly corrected itself.

I remember rocking up to her ward, her bed, seeing the curtains drawn and hearing voices on the other side talking soothingly to Mum. Anxiety and terror weighed heavily on me at that moment. What was I about to enter into?

What was I about to see on the other side of the curtain? A big part of me didn't want to know. I wanted to run! And then I remembered that it was Mum on the other side, and whatever event or experience was about to unfold, I needed to be there to support her. Imagine how terrified she must be feeling. I braced myself, stepped up to the curtain, and pulled it back.

I was 41 years old and yet felt like I was growing up in that moment into a fully-fledged adult. As I walked through the curtains, knowing it was time to take charge, I said, "Hello, my name is Michele, and that's my mum. How can I help?"

It was a long couple of days in the hospital. We came and went and hoped for the best. Mum couldn't talk, though she seemed aware, so all we could do was make her as comfortable as we could as we waited for the doctors to move through the steps of healing her.

I remember the last night we saw her in the hospital. She was sitting on the bed, and my son was sitting on a chair not too far away from her. They had a close and special relationship. She started leaning forward. I wondered what was going on. Did she need help? It took the longest while, as if every effort was being made by her to take this action, which resulted in her kissing my son's cheek.

I don't know if she knew, but it turned out my son was the last person my mum kissed in this life. The following morning, I answered a knock at my door to find my dad and brother on the other end. Mum had suffered a massive stroke during the night and was gone.

Mum had died.

I was shattered. It was such a shock! And therein began the emotional journey that I had dreamed about. I was locked in now to the grieving journey, and I had to remember to breathe.

The funeral was another step up for me. We had lost my youngest brother in a car accident when I was 27 years old, and at that time, although I wrote the eulogy for my brother's funeral, I wasn't brave enough to deliver it. I had felt regretful about that ever since, so at Mum's funeral, I was determined to speak up for her. My fear and anxiety about public speaking were pushed to the side, and I wrote and spoke the eulogy from the heart, speaking for my mum in the way she deserved to be spoken about. She was a stalwart woman with a strong sense of loyalty and duty, and I was completely unafraid at that moment to express my grief, vulnerability, and distress at losing my umbilical cord to life.

After that, the healing began. Mum's death had been sudden, unexpected, and traumatic for me. Fortunately, I have a strong spiritual belief system and I believe in reincarnation. I believe that we are souls who incarnate into physical form, time and again, to learn, evolve, and fulfill a meaningful purpose. I believe that when we leave this life, we go down the birth canal into some other existence, some other world. Due to this, after Mum died, I remember saying, "Mum, if there is such a thing as an afterlife, then you'll let me know with a sign". Growing up in South Africa, the memory that stood out for me, from long weekend drives in the car, was a song on the radio that I loved – 'Tie a Yellow Ribbon Around the Old Oak Tree'.

Mum, when I hear that song, I'll know you're okay and that an afterlife does exist.

I forgot all about this pact until six or so months later. We used to play Buzz all the time when the kids were little, a music game where you guessed the name or artist of a song and had to do so quickly if you wanted to win. We'd played it many, many times before, but on this night one of the options to choose from was 'Tie a Yellow Ribbon Around the Old Oak Tree'. As soon as I saw it, I remembered the sign I had asked Mum for, and it prompted me to say to my brother Julian,

"Can you believe that when Mum died, I asked for a sign? I said it would be "Tie a Yellow

Ribbon Around the Old Oak Tree". And there it is.'

Julian replied, 'Well, how funny is that? Because today I was rifling through all my old records and I came across that song and played it.'

Goosebumps. I felt assured at that moment that it was a message from my mother telling me that she was okay and that an afterlife does exist.

Some other woo-woo experiences that were incredible after Mum died included how my mum's name kept appearing everywhere. Her name was Hilda, and whilst she was alive, I never heard or saw that name anywhere, let alone meet anyone named Hilda. After she died, when a new group of Tarot students started at the College, one of them was named Hilda. I remember quickly ducking into a group of shops to purchase some supplies for my niece's 10th birthday, and as I rounded the corner there was a café in that section called Hilda. I was also channel surfing one night, watching two movies at the same time, and just happened upon a scene in the movie that showed the outside of a movie theatre – and the first name of the actor on the advertising banner at the top was Hilda!

These signs were all reassuring and helped me heal somewhat through the grieving process. It made me feel hopeful about a future that wouldn't include my mum in physical form but suggested she would always be there or around me energetically.

I had other tools in my spiritual wellness healing kit, too, as I had been in the field since my twenties and knew to exercise mindset strategies and practice gratitude, and I also reached out for counselling to deal with my grieving emotions. I was lucky, too, that I had a 10-year-old boy to take care of. He got me out of bed every morning. Mum used to say the devil finds work for idle hands. I was grateful that I had a family to care for and work to keep me busy and purposeful, and I nurtured myself gently through the grieving process with many mindset tools.

I also practiced gratitude every single day. Every single day I missed my mum. The gap she left in my life was cold and vast, and I felt that grief every single day. It hurt. It was heartbreaking. And I cried and cried if I had to. After that, I was then grateful. I had lost my mum, but my son was still here, my dad was still here, my brother, his children, my sister-in-law, and friends were all still here. I was still surrounded by much life, love, and support.

I deliberately shifted my perspective as I mourned the loss of my mother every single day. I always felt grateful for all the life that was still left in mine. I believe that, with grief, you don't get over it. You just find a way to move past or evolve beyond it. The grief of losing a loved one is always there. I love this graphic with the balls of grief. It shows us that the size of grief doesn't change, but we can grow a bigger life around grief through self-healing, self-nurturing, and self-love.

People tend to believe that grief shrinks over time

What really happens is that we grow around our grief

Grief is different, too, for everybody, and there's no use by or end date on our grief. We all have our grieving path, and if anything is the same it should be that we never give up on finding the healing path that's just right for us.

For me, being grateful every single day for the life still here helped me mourn the loss of my mum's life proactively and positively. Three to four years down the track, when zest and zeal returned to my life, I believed that it was my daily practice of gratitude, whilst grieving, that helped me to feel lighter and brighter than ever before.

Que Sera Sera is a grieving with gratitude story, and in your accompanying journal, you can heal through your chapter of loss and heartache in the form of a letter to your loved one.

On each page you will find various journal prompts to invoke memories and provide space for you to express gratitude for who they were, what they did, and how they impacted your life. Also, learn about the four tasks of grief, be shown how to create a grieving ritual, and recognise comforting signs and proof of life from loved ones. They haven't abandoned us; they have simply changed their form.

Namaste,

Chapter 5

Vanessa Cirocco

Transformation after trauma

TRIGGER WARNING

Themes of sexual assault and domestic violence are stated in this story. PTSD is challenging and if you're going through that, you are strong; you will get through this. If you know someone going through it, you don't need to have all the answers; be supportive and compassionate the best way you know how. Also, don't be afraid to ask for help and look after yourself, too. Help is always available.

It all started when I was around 18 years old – my life was shaken up and everything was about to change!

"Go back to your girlfriend," I said after he placed his grubby hands on my leg. He smelled of liquor, and my body froze, shocked at what was happening. I thought, he's drunk, he's probably just confused. He proceeded to lift my shirt; I said 'GO AWAY!' but he was persistent. Afterwards, I watched him walk away. I couldn't move; my eyes slowly shut, and I drifted off to sleep.

The next morning, I opened my eyes, I thought, and I hoped that it had been a bad dream. I heard the door open and my heart started racing. I saw his face, and he aggressively blurted out the words, "You better not tell my girlfriend." I heard the shower running; his partner was in there.

I felt detached from my body as I left the house. I was so confused, lost, and had no idea how to handle the situation. He was confronted, a couple of weeks later, his lip quivering, scared. He could sense my vulnerability; I was only young, and he thought I wouldn't tell anyone. Eventually he ended up telling people that I was the reason he did what he did. The people that surrounded me didn't care. Said things like, "Why didn't she scream?" and "Why didn't she say anything earlier?" These were the people I thought cared about me, who I thought would have my back, but this situation reflected where they were at.

It showed up in later years, when I realised I had a lot of wounds to heal. I was let down by the ones I thought I could rely on the most.

Fast forward a year or so later, I got into a relationship. At first, this partner helped me a lot on my journey. We went on adventures, we had fun, and it was a great distraction from everything I was going through. I still feel like crap about the situation but never actually did anything to deal with it. This was at a time before the #metoo movement came about; no one was talking about anything regarding sexual assault. Plus, I was only young, and at this stage I didn't know how to ask for help or what to do about it. I was lost, felt completely unsupported, and had never felt so alone. Things were pretty good in the relationship; obviously, like any relationship, it had its difficult moments, but nothing out of the ordinary – or so I thought. Then one night, again, alcohol was consumed, and a miscommunication happened. It was like time was slowing and speeding up at the same time. His hand had contacted my face. I was shocked. My body reacted in a way it had never performed before. I had never been able to run so quickly; my brain knew exactly what to do, sending me running out of the house and finding people in front of their house, I explained the situation, and my partner proceeded to follow me. In the middle of the conversation with them, I suddenly bolted back to the house, locked him out, and contacted people for help. Thanks to adrenaline, I was able to keep myself safe.

Afterwards, I felt my body break. My soul felt like it was gone. I know now that I hadn't healed from my first traumatic event, and this second event brought me to a breaking point. I was at my lowest; I didn't know what was happening and I had no idea what to do. I didn't know why these things kept happening to me. I felt like I couldn't hold on any longer; I didn't want to do life anymore. I was stuck. Time stood still. I was acting recklessly and spent time with people who didn't have my best intentions at heart. There was a lot of partying, and a LOT of drinking. I was constantly trying to find an escape, battling a big, dark cloud hanging over my head. I had broken into pieces.

Then, I locked myself in my house for six months and didn't want to leave. The people in my life didn't know what to do, either. I had never felt so alone in the world. I couldn't understand reality anymore; nothing looked the same. I didn't know who I was. I couldn't face people, and when I did, I froze. I couldn't even look at myself in the mirror. I couldn't look at the world and not think negatively. I couldn't see the good in anything – everything looked dark and gloomy. I couldn't make sense of simple things.

After going through these traumas, and other negative experiences. After constantly having emotional breakdowns and experiencing life that felt uncomfortable. I knew something had to change. I decided I needed help. I went to therapy, and I finally received the help I didn't know how to ask for. I started doing new things and using the tools they gave me. This started my personal development journey. I was reading so many personal development books, delving deep into myself and trying to make sense of it all. Having a bit of faith helped the process. I realised I must want the change for myself; no one else could do it for me. There were guides, mentors, belief systems, but I was the one who had to put in the work. Even just a tiny bit of hope made a world of difference. As someone who has seen and been through some terrible things – yeah, sure, some have it worse, some have it better, but none of that matters when you're deep in depression – I knew I had a little something, the tiniest spark to ignite, and that's what I held on to. During this time, I was having multiple breakdowns, becoming easily offended by small things, constantly triggered. Looking back, I have to say, these are the typical reactions for someone who's experienced trauma.

I slowly started getting myself back out into the world, doing things I used to love and trying new things. This started some momentum to my healing even though I still felt terrible. I would try to be proud of myself, but it was still hard. During this time, I did things that got me out of my comfort zone. That alone time was crucial, though. I needed deep rest; my soul yearned for it. Therapists told me that I needed to get out, so I pushed myself. Balance is so important. From there, things started to look up a little bit more each time from a breakdown.

What I've learnt from the inner work is, healing isn't so straightforward. It's not easy, it's not pretty – it's messy. There were things that came up that I needed to heal. I started walking more, started focusing on my health. It felt like it was working a bit, but I hadn't noticed any big changes. One day I came across practicing gratitude. I had never heard about it in my life; growing up as a child in the 90s, it wasn't talked about, so it was a whole new concept for me to take onboard. I remember the early days of when I started healing, sitting there writing in my notebook about the things I was grateful for. I would write about my dog, the people I did have supporting me, material possessions, access to food and water.

From there, my reality started shifting! I would go on walks before this because I knew I had to do activities that would assist me in feeling better, but after practicing gratitude, I started noticing more. I noticed the trees, the grass, flowers, birds. Things that were there before but I hadn't been seeing. I noticed I didn't have to do these activities – I got to do these things. I had legs, and my body did so much for me, even after everything it had been through. And I'm alive!

Along my journey, I have reflected on the past (before the trauma) and realised I've always liked the things in my life but never really taken the time to intentionally appreciate them. I started wondering if this was how I got to where I am now. I started understanding everything. The more I practiced gratitude, the more I noticed; when I went for walks, I noticed the colour of the flowers, the grain of the bark in the trees. Everything was becoming brighter and better.

I can't discredit everything else I was doing during this healing time, but the one thing I can continuously return to is gratitude. Therapy is great! I don't regret a thing about it and would highly recommend it to others. But in the world we live in, not everyone has the means to access it frequently. The beautiful thing about gratitude is that it's free! We can access it from anywhere, at any time, and in any moment. It has become a way of being for me. Yeah, I went through a lot of traumas, but I know now, it was a wakeup call. I consider myself blessed sometimes; okay, yeah, life may have turned out differently if it hadn't happened to me, but that's because it happened for me. Before I was just going about life, doing whatever I wanted, whatever I felt like. I don't think I was a bad person prior to these events, but I don't think I ever considered others as much as I do now, I didn't understand others as much as I do now, I didn't see the world like I do now, I didn't care about the earth at all compared to how I do now, I didn't appreciate the beauty of things that were right in front of me compared to what I do now. I started becoming more open and receptive to life, which meant new opportunities, people, and experiences started flowing into my life.

Essentially, gratitude changed me in more ways than one; I didn't even think it would have this much of an impact when I first started. I was like, 'Oh, cool, a little activity that I can do that might make me feel a bit better.' Gratitude isn't just writing a list of things that you're grateful for to get more in life. It's a spiritual experience to better health and wellbeing, a mind, body, and spirit connection. It's not just I'm happy that I have these things, so I'm going to write down what I'm grateful for so I can get more. Each to their own – if material possessions make you sustainably happy, go for it. I know that wasn't the case for me. It's being grateful for the life we have all been blessed with, it's appreciating the beauty of nature all around us, it's seeing the good in people, it's taking moments to slow down and look at everything you have around you and not taking that for granted! We are all connected. There is so much to be grateful for. Even when you have fewer material possessions, you have life! The material possessions you have, do you take them for granted, or are you grateful for them? I realised I couldn't manifest more of what I want if I'm not grateful for what I already have. Why would the universe reward me like that? That was a hard pill to swallow, but it's the one that made the most impact for me.

Further along the journey, you begin to notice how other people aren't grateful. I place no judgement on them; after all, I was one of them. It's good to remember where you've come from and how much you've changed! It's important to stand grounded in your gratitude. You'll notice, there will be others who engage in low vibrational conversation. Allow them – it's not your job to change anyone. What I have found really empowering is seeing people in my life, noticing the little things in life. They will be like wow, did you see the sky tonight? Did you the see the moon? That sets my soul on fire. Knowing I am making an impact, helping others notice what they may have forgotten and remembering how beautiful the little things really are. The beautiful sunsets that light the skies with pinks, purples, and oranges. The moon. The sun that does so much for us, our health, and the planet. If we start expanding from within, I know it's going to have a ripple effect on everyone around us.

The change starts within you!

This didn't happen overnight for me: I'm on a healing journey. I have had to delve deep into the darkest parts of myself to realise things I had been missing, to heal myself, to grow. That involved unpacking all the trauma I went through. I stopped distracting myself and putting all my energy to others and started giving back to myself. I haven't done this alone; I have worked with others along the way. This is why I do the work I do; I felt so alone, but if I didn't have the people I was so lucky to be blessed with when I reached out, I don't know where I would be now.

Do you feel like you are stuck, lost, or often wonder "Why does this happen to me?" You're not alone. I've had so many 'AH-HA!" moments. When there is an uncomfortable feeling or I was feeling triggered, I chose to listen, instead of ignore; I ended up grateful, grateful for myself for putting in the work, grateful for not ignoring it, grateful for it coming up so I could heal it. This is how you take the power back. THIS IS WHEN LIFE STARTS TO UNFOLD. This is when I started finding the beauty in it all. You can, too. Everyone has the ability to tap into themselves. No one knows you better than you know yourself, no matter how lost you are FEELING or in those moments when you are lost. Even when you are lost, it's a moment to find a way back to yourself and even discover new aspects of yourself along the way. This is the journey of alchemy. It can be difficult but is incredibly rewarding, and I am so grateful for it.

This journey has also led me to a new career path: I now help others help themselves. I am at a place where I have gratitude for the people who hurt me. It was not okay, but I am grateful for how they helped me realise my true purpose on this planet. We all have the power inside of us to change our entire reality. We are constantly creating how our lives go. If you're here, no matter where you are on your journey, there is always something to be grateful for.

On my journey, I have realised how life is full of ups and downs. This is the method that I use to do the inner work!

Release and reflect

Mind dump! Journal everything you are feeling and wanting to let go of. You can do this to reflect on anything in the present or to reflect on your past to visit some things that you feel may be holding onto that and holding you back. GET IT ALL OUT! It doesn't need to be perfect; no need to stress about perfect grammar. You're taking everything going on your mind, taking that energy coming down though your arm, out of the pen, and putting it onto the paper. You may notice here thoughts that no longer serve you; you may find things that you didn't even realise you were holding on to. It's a great way to reflect, see what is going on, and affirm, 'I choose to let this go.'

Practice gratitude

Writing a list of what you are grateful is great for shifting your perspective. If you're feeling great, you'll probably find it easy to find more things to be grateful for. If life has been testing you, as it does many of us, you may find it a bit more challenging, which is why it's such a great practice. When you start being grateful, you find even more things to be grateful for. You can reflect on what you released when you journaled about whether it was a negative or positive experience. Is there anything you can take from the what you journaled? You can be grateful for things you have realised about yourself or other people. You can also list other things that you are grateful for in the present moment. What can you see around you? It can be as simple as being grateful for yourself for making time for this practice. Once you have a list, place your hand over your heart, read what you are grateful for, and feel it into your heart space. This will help open your heart chakra, which leads you to be more receptive to having even more gratitude and better experiences. It all starts within!

Positive affirmations

Once you have released what no longer serves you and have practiced gratitude, you can implement positive affirmations of how you want to show up in the world. If you noticed on reflecting that some traits or feelings don't serve you, this is the place to manifest how you want to be. A quick little tip: when journaling or feeling emotions, it's great to say I feel sad instead of I am sad. Whenever you put, 'I am' in front of what you say, you are identifying with it and claiming it as yours. That's why using positive affirmations is so incredibly powerful! You accept that you feel sad: 'I feel sad.' Really feel it; be grateful for it showing up to show you what you need to feel and then releasing it. Then replace it with a positive affirmation, for example, "I am happy."

Chapter 6

Jodie Eustice

Be the fabulous You! One's inner self journey

Gratitude should not be just a reaction to getting what you want, but an ALL-THE-TIME gratitude, the kind where you notice the little things and where you constantly look for the good, even in unpleasant situations, start bringing gratitude to your experiences, instead of waiting for a positive experience in order to feel grateful. – Marelisa Fàrega

I am very lucky to live on a hill with a view from both the front veranda and back deck. I seek out the morning sun on the front veranda, especially in winter, when there are glorious, colourful sunrises. Afternoons are spent on the back deck with lovely views of treetops and distant hills with homes etched onto them. This is where I can see the changing sunset colours as the sun fades behind the hill into the darkness of night and the lights start to flicker in the distant city. The back deck is one of most tranquil zen space I have created. I retreat to this space in the afternoon in the cooler months, as the sun starts to warm the area. Today, the black and white magpie-lark is splashing around in the bird bath, the doves are in the bird feeder, and a while earlier I was entertained by the rainbow lorikeets with their funny antics and vibrant feathers.

Sitting on my back deck this afternoon, it is a clear blue sunny day with the odd puffy cloud moving in the distance from the high wind. They float along peacefully in the sky. It is so relaxing to watch them drift by, watching their shapes form and change continually as they pass across the sky. It reminds me of being a child, lying on the coolness of green couch grass, looking for animal-shaped clouds.

A gentle breeze rustles the leaves in the tall liquid amber tree in my next-door neighbour's backyard. Enjoyment of their magnificent tree without having the maintenance makes it easy to love it, to appreciate what it gives to our area, as a safe place for birds and wildlife to be protected by its size, by the shade provided by its height. The tree is surprisingly still filled with mostly green leaves, with the flicker of brownie orange colours changing at the start of winter. Soon it will be just bare branches. Those brown dry leaves will provide nutrients back to the earth below. So, for a few more weeks, I will enjoy this beautiful tree till it is just bare branches. Then it will give me a different view, to see the sunset colours more through the branches normally hidden behind fully laden branches of leaves.

The sound changes through the leaves as the rhythm of the wind shifts from stillness with no breeze to a symphony playing as the wind picks up, entering the canopy of the trees, peaks and troughs, quietness to loud, swaying jostle. If I close my eyes, I can listen to the leaves' music as they play their song for me. I feel the sensation of the wind on my body. It makes the hairs on my arms rise as goose bumps grow up out of my skin from the coolness in the air.

Then the wind stops; the sun starts to warm me back up, so that my skin goes back to its ageing, freckly normality, till the next gash of wind comes through and my senses are heightened again – and back up go those goose bumps. I feel quite alive in this moment.

The butterfly wind chime hanging on the back deck gently clangs in the background. I'm happy I bought it, as I'm now reminded of my adventure with my cousin to the sunflower field and an impromptu trip for lunch at our favourite nursery and cafe in Warwick. It's another memory I treasure in my heart, of time spent with her, of our day trip and fun in the sunflower field, taking photographs for my next project of Sunflower Bliss Oracle Cards (another goal, aspiration, and dream to fulfil).

This is just a small part of what I feel gratitude for in my life. Outside for 30 minutes, I am so grateful for being able to sit here, to be able to acknowledge that I can see the beauty in the little things that I experience in life. The list of things to be grateful for is so variable and is always changing, just as life is always changing, so it can be quite a long list of things that bring joy into my life or things that I have created in my life. I am also joyful that I sit here with gratitude for myself, in myself now.

But there have been times when it wasn't always like this for me: this appreciating the beauty in life, the practicing of gratitude in the little things, seeing the world with positivity from an open, loving heart.

I grew up in the 1970s in a small country town. I have so many wonderful memories of my childhood. Time spent chasing soldier crabs on the front beach, fishing off the jetty, the excitement of the yearly show, going on the rides, water pistol fights in the main street on festival weekend, spending time at the pool to cool off in the summer heat, mango juice running down my arms – I have so many good childhood memories. Even now, whenever I go home for a visit, my connection to my hometown is still strong.

My mum was 18 when she got married to my dad, and I came along that same year. My beautiful mother is from a family of eight kids. There was a lot of love in this family for each other, and there still is. My grandma's love was as comforting as an endless packet of ginger kisses to all of us in our family. My dad was five years older, an only child, surrounded by cousins and the odd foster child looked after by his Catholic parents. Jack, my grandad, was a quiet man who smelt like rollie cigarettes; he would tap his tobacco-stained fingers on the table for hours on end, lost in his own thoughts, probably trying to keep the peace in the house that he built. My grandmother shared her love of old-time movies with me, so we spent many hours watching dancing beauties in glamorous gowns, singing tunes while being spun around by tuxedo dapper handsome man or western movies, where *Calamity Jane* became my all-time favourite movie.

My dad... for some reason I idolised him as a little girl. He was my hero. It's so hard to put into words why I felt this way about him, but I'm sure most little girls adore their dads. I had a connection with my dad, an unexplainable connection.

As a young girl, I have so many good memories where I felt safe. When I was at preschool, my dad would pick me up at lunchtime on his push bike; he would be as black as the ace of spades with soot on his entire body from working in the coke works. And I would sit proudly on the metal bar between his arms riding home, feeling safe. I would go everywhere with him. But this also meant I spent a lot of time alone outside one of the many pubs in town, waiting hours for him, begging him to come home while sitting in a hot car. On weekends, so I could spend time with him, I would go with him whenever he was working on the farms or cattle stations.

One of my fondest memories spent with my dad is him waking me up in the early hours in the mornings to take me to the stables. We would pick up his racehorse Oscar – *Who Dares Win* – to go to the beach. I would watch him go do beach work with Oscar, sitting on the sand dune in darkness as they cantered off into the distance, out of sight. Waiting for their return, I would watch the sunrise over the ocean, coming up over the horizon, the colours of the sky changing into lightness while listening to the waves gently crash onto the golden sand. In the distance you could hear the galloping hooves pound the sand, with the heavy breathing of the horse as it was worked. This is my special place to go to when I want to remember my dad. That memory is a gift from Dad that I am grateful for.

But there are many more memories that have brought a lot of heartache; they are the ones that are painful when remembered. My dad had his own unhealed story. He was the cross-eyed bastard, as he would call himself. Sometimes as kids, my brother and I wouldn't know who was in trouble because of his eye condition; I know he joked about it, but it was something that made him different, too. A great sense of humour was his way of deal with his own demons, I think; he could also be a bit of a smart-ass larrikin.

As a teenager on a cricket field, my dad found out he was adopted; from what I have been told, this affected him at the time. Looking back in reflection now, I can see he suffered from mental health issues all of his life, and his abuse of alcohol was part of his coping mechanism. With that, his unhealed life impacted on my life from the day I was born till he committed suicide in 1989. Even now there are things that I will be triggered by because of him.

That Father's Day, my dad made a choice – a devastating choice. His choice ultimately impacted him, but it also impacted others that he loved in his life in varying ways. I can only share how his choice impacted my life.

I deeply love my dad, and I will truly miss him till the day I die. Forgiveness has taken a lot of time and has involved different emotions ranging from hate, to anger, to sadness, as well as the release of my own inner guilt by seeking professional counselling over the years and doing my own ongoing inner healing work. But I am honest in saying, with a loving heart, that I'm grateful my dad is at peace. I am grateful my family has a different life without him. I am grateful we don't have to live with his unhealed agony from his mental health, alcohol abuse, and self-worth issues anymore. Most importantly, I am grateful for that he is free of his darkness.

My dad worked hard; even on the days he was hungover, he would still go to work. Dad had a very short temper; he could be quite verbally abusive. At times I was a verbal punching bag to him, as were my mother and brother. This came quite easily to him, putting me down with cruel, hurtful comments and belittling remarks. There were many times we would flee from our home when he was in one of his volatile states, hurling toxic verbal abuse. My mum would remove us from our home when she could to protect us, especially when he was in a state of jealous, frightening rage, as she just couldn't trust if he would turn physical – there was always that fear. It was quite scary for all of us. While I don't remember being physically abused, we did know the wrath of his leather belt or the back of his hand if we were naughty, so probably now that is classed as physical abuse. It isn't what I remember it as or how I think it was even now.

For a child growing up in this environment, it can be quite confusing. One minute my dad was someone I loved so very much; the next minute he was scaring me, hurting my heart, breaking my spirit as well as so many promises he made to me were broken. Living with a personality where you didn't know what you were going to get on a daily basis was really hard. A lot of time was spent tiptoeing around his emotional state. I spent a lot of my childhood particularly my teenage years in my bedroom, so I could hide away, reading and listening to music to block the draining energy from outside the door. There was no way I could have any friends come over to visit as I didn't want the risk of being embarrassed, so I spent a lot of time on my own.

As a child growing up in an unsafe and frightening environment, I had to adapt my personality to protect myself from emotional hurt and fearful feelings. When my dad drank, there could be two different types of personalities to come out. Sometimes it was the loving dad who let his guard down and told me he loved me, loved us; then there was the unreasonable, angry man who I didn't want to be near for fear and humiliation of what he might do. In those situations, it was like I had to control my being – what I did, what I said, who I was – so it wouldn't make him angry or want to drink more.

My dad probably didn't have the mental capacity to understand that what he was living was projecting down to his child. I somehow learnt these skills growing up in this situation, and those protection skills have become part of my personality traits. Feeling as though I had to be always had to be in control and mature has transitioned into my adulthood. With any relationships, whether family, partner, or friendships, there is always a fear of doing or saying the wrong thing with a deep dread of upsetting people, of letting them down. I have people-pleasing behaviours, where I want to make others happy, so they will want me in their life, so they will like/love me. Always questioning whether I'm good enough, seeking external validation from others because of my own lack of self-worth.

At times I wonder what life would be like if my dad had been a different person, if I had had a different life. Daydreaming became my way of escaping as a child. When I was in high school, I would often daydream about being rescued. That Boy George would take me away in his limousine to a better life. Ironically, I realise now I picked the wrong 1980s pop icon to save me. I even daydreamed about worst case scenarios at times, but never did I ever think that something so tragic would ever happen to our family. As an adult, I daydream less now. But when I'm in a bad place mentally, it's something I do to take me away from the present.

One of my recurring joyful daydreams was what my life would be like as a mother. As a little girl, I loved playing with my dolls and our pets, pretending they were my babies, playing house and visualising having my own family, a loving husband, and a white picket fence house.

Sometimes you make choices in life. Some were the right choice at the time, some were the wrong choice, and others weren't your choice at all. I married young in my 20s; while a family was what we wanted, it didn't happen. Then I spent quite a few years on my own in my 30s, discovering myself. That was one of the right choices I made. I'm grateful for my 30s, as this was when I discovered who I was meant to be at that time of my life. Independent, confidence, assertive; I finally became ME. I met my partner/best friend in my late 30s. Some choices mean your life alters; you may sacrifice how you think your life will be from your childhood dreams. For me, the choice of not having a child has taken my life in a different and yet *wonderful* direction. But sometimes I do feel sadness for not being a mother, for not experiencing the joy of having a family like I dreamt about as a little girl. That sadness has made me grieve at times, for a different life that wasn't meant to be.

Sometimes you have to let of the picture of what you thought it would be like and learn to find joy in the story you are actually living.

– Rachel Marie Martin

I have struggled on and off over my 52 years with depression, anxiety, even feeling like the black sheep because I have sensed and felt I am different from others. I have also struggled with my weight for majority of my life. This has created a lifelong disappointment in myself. My emotional relationship with food has been something that I have battle with throughout life, and it started to creep back in over the last few years.

Turning 50 in 2020, I was starting to go to a bad dark place. I questioned whether it was my second midlife crisis?

I'm well on other side of menopause now, realising that I'm heading into my golden crone years with my wonderful partner, but no family connection since we don't have children of our own is a lonely thought. I also started experiencing some physical health issues along with chronic exhaustion that further aggravated my mental health issues. Then, coping with pandemic stresses has thrown me into a dark vortex.

It was like my body, mind, and soul were not in alignment; they definitely weren't working together in harmony. I had a mental breakdown in 2020, then another in 2021, which was a doozy where I started heading down the path of evaluating my dad's final choice. It was really scaring me, the heavy feeling of being so connected to him, of starting to understand/ resonate with his darkness before he committed suicide. I thought I was going CRAZY! I was really questioning the essence of my being. What was my value of being here? What was my purpose? It was like I needed to understand facets of who I was and why the hell I was like this. I decide to delve deeper into my spiritual mindfulness to understand what was causing my anxiety, ongoing exhaustion, and spiralling self-worth. Why was I feeling this way?

So, I went within to understand my story. By isolating myself at the time as it was easy for me to retreat within when I was in my anxious existence. But I also knew I had to reach out to my partner, family and understanding friends to let them know that I was struggling. I sought out professional help from my doctor, life coach, and naturopath to support me in this period as well as healing modalities like Reiki and Access Bars.

With a lot of inner work, I realised that I am triggered by broken promises and that I have unclear boundaries with myself. I started to understand that some of the programming in my coping abilities stems from unhealed trauma. My own unhealed childhood trauma has triggered unexplained emotions. And the self-preservation traits that have protected me in the past have actually become a hindrance to me now. I have created a lot of limiting beliefs in myself and they are a burden to which I was clinging.

I am grateful I was intrigued to find answers. That part of my mindfulness journey was seeking out self-reflection, nurturing myself with self-love practice, and learning to have self-acceptance, along with incorporating achievable daily self-care routines by doing small things like moisturising my body, taking my supplements, listening to meditations, finding joy in small things like nature, and journaling my thoughts of gratitude.

On this ongoing spiritual mindfulness journey, there have been many aha moments that have opened my eyes. I know, if I'm being truly honest with myself, that at times I am so conditioned to my anxiety. It has always been there. The anxiety of living with unhealed childhood trauma and being always in a heightened nervous state as a child. This is part of my identity that I try to hide in; it is my coping mechanism to protect myself from being hurt from others.

At times, it is also my resistance to heal from my own bullshit, too. Yes, life has had some bullshit moments, but it also has had so many more wonderful, fun-filled, fabulous moments. Lately, I have let some hard bullshit moments, whether with work or life in general, catch me by surprise, and then I spiral into an exhausted state where I just can't cope. Trying to find the energy to climb out of that exhaustion is hard. But there is a person in there who is really fun; I know she would rather be the one up for an adventure, the one who likes to laugh, dance, and sing, the one who pushes herself to do a challenge, the one who wants to explore the world, and the one surrounded by others. But now, when I become aware of what I'm doing and am ready to see it, I breathe, acknowledge it, and show myself some compassion. Inner work healing is an ongoing process, but it is so worth it.

Somehow, healing knew all along that I was on my way to her. I am grateful that she waited for me.

– Parm Kaur

In 2017, I started journaling as part of my working on the *"fabulous me"* spiritual journey; I thought writing down my anxious thoughts would help me to see reason in my unclear thinking. Doing this is where I started to capture what I was grateful for in my life. I would write my feelings down, but also describe them in poems and record any relevant and meaningful quotes I found on social media. Journaling became part of a daily practice as my commitment to my self-care, as did incorporating other tools from the spiritual medicine box, like using essential oils, oracle cards, crystals, reading copious self-help books, going to women's circles and art and craft workshops, and seeking healing services from others and guided meditation into my healing journey.

I took a further deep dive with medium readings to connect with spirit, most importantly my dad, who came through, which helped provide some closure. I love to learn; I'm a Sagittarius, so studying my astrology natal chart helped me to understand more about my personality traits, as well as numerology and about how the moon phases can affect the energies surrounding me. It was like a new world of learning, and I found it so fascinating to pinpoint how different modalities connect the dots on where I start to make sense of who I am and what my beliefs and values are. Understanding myself has been a very rewarding quest.

This spiritual journey, along with practicing gratitude, has been a saving grace when I wasn't in the best place mentally. Especially when I was thinking I wanted to be in eternal darkness. So, I'm grateful that I was able to push forward with daily practice of gratitude, meditation, affirmations, and journaling. Even now, I journal and use a gratitude app to record what I'm grateful for each day. I aim to find three things that I am grateful for; some days are easy to enter in my daily gratitude, but other days aren't. On those hard days, I may enter something I'm grateful for, like:

- my journal
- I woke up
- I went to work
- sunflowers
- the sky is blue
- my little dog, Maisie, wants to be near me always
- my friend sent me a SMS, so I know I'm on their mind
- my partner
- morning coffee
- I have a home

Gratitude to me is found in the small things, from simple gestures from others, the feeling when you experience love and warmth around you. It's seeing the beauty in life, appreciating the magnificence of nature, knowing there is meaning to life by being present, acknowledging that there is so much value in life. There is purpose in being here, and by being able to see, feel, hear, sense, and smell all that this universe is providing for you. Being grateful is a unique but simple practice.

Has being grateful and expressing gratitude helped me? Hell yes; I'm more a glass half-full person to a full-glass person on most days. Though there are still many times I'm running on an empty glass, too. There is a balance; it isn't always perfect in life. There are days where retreating back into my exhaustive darkness comes quite easily, sometimes unexpectedly so. But knowing I have the ability to venture out of an exhaustion state with some rest, using my self-care practices, and allowing a lot of compassion for myself gives solace.

I still have so much work to do on myself. To be honest, I know I probably always will; healing oneself is an ongoing process. Yes, it gets tiring at times. On those exhausting days, when I'm ready, I acknowledge that feeling, accept that some parts of me will be triggered to go back to traits ingrained from childhood. But I know now it will pass. On the good days, I appreciate that I'm evolving, learning more about my inner workings, using tools to guide me in the direction needed to be healed. Learning more about yourself opens you up to endless possibilities of what further potential is in your life to be experienced along with self-improvement and self-love. Even writing this chapter has been a part of my healing process. I had to really go within, revisit some hard and forgotten memories, purge difficult emotions, and release varying feelings as well as let go of the limiting stories I have been telling myself and living within all my life.

Most importantly, having gratitude for life is important for knowing your self-worth, which I recognise is part of my healing journey. So today I'm grateful for my life, I am grateful I add value to the ones I love, I am grateful for the family and friends who want to be part of my life in the good times and they accept me in the dark times. Most importantly, I am grateful for being ME, the fabulous, quirky me.

Dad, I am here.
Are you still with me?
Or are you elsewhere?

I need me to be here,
Didn't you want to be here too?

Be where you want,
Just let me be!

And you will be a memory I will forever kept.

– Jodie Eustice, 3/09/2022

In loving memory of Ronald John Eustice
5 September 1947 – 3 September 1989 (Father's Day)
I promised you I will never forget you, and I haven't.

Chapter 7

Taryn Claire Le Nu

To my beloved gratitude

To my beloved Gratitude

This is my ode to you. A long overdue acknowledgement of a dear and beloved companion. I believe that it's not where you are in life that matters, but rather who you have by your side – and darling Gratitude, you have proven to be a most exemplary partner to travel through life with.

Each and every day, you serve me well, and I serve you.

I fell in love with you when I realised that you were the single thing I could control in any given moment, when so much else was outside of my scope of control. Time has taught me that walking this life with you by my side has given me the enormous ability to unlock the fullness of life, turning scratchy problems into gifts and failures into successes. You've taught me to concentrate on finding and extracting the good in every single situation. You've helped me discover that my life was filled with opportunities for even more gratitude. As I created more awareness of these opportunities to invite you further in, the feelings produced then nurtured my very soul.

Gratitude, you are indeed the antidote to negative emotions.

The neutraliser of envy, hostility, worry, and irritation.

You are the savouring, the *not* taking things for granted.

You, my beautiful friend, are in-the-moment, present-oriented, where fear and anxiety hold no charge.

When I do my daily "Gratitude grabs" with you, it genuinely helps me make sense of my past and ultimately brings me peace for tomorrow. Spending formal time with you each day helps set the co-ordinates for creating a vision for my future. Spending informal time with you during the day tweaks small moments in time, sprinkling them with sparkles and making those moments come alive.

I joke to my friends about your attitude, dearest Gratitude. The Attitude of Gratitude is a great little rhyme, but I am equal witness to the rewards when it is followed as a way of life. When I am grateful for the things I have (thankful for those things both great and small), it fills and permeates my life in a positive way. Harnessing your wonderful attitude has incredible repercussions, making things feel super special while opening the door to the power, wisdom, and creativity of the universe.

You, my beloved Gratitude, are the key that opens the door.

I have to tell you, my beloved Gratitude, that when I am with you, crazy shifts happen. In all honesty, I can say that fear disappears and abundance appears. How do you do that? When I started noticing the effect you had on me, I leaned in closer and whispered, "Show me more of the magic that you perform". You did not disappoint. The more of your magic shows that I attended, the more magical my life became. In childlike wonder I heard the background music of my life change beat; I witnessed the curtain sweep back and a full beaming spotlight luminesce the stage of my life.

Doris Day had you sussed right from the get-go when she recognised you for what you truly are and acknowledged all that you are responsible for "Gratitude is riches. Complaint is poverty". It stopped me in my tracks. I learnt to catch myself and put a halt to that dirty little C word.

I've lain with my head in your lap while we conversed for hours. I've taken on your advice to developing my own Attitude of Gratitude and give thanks for everything that is happening *for* me.

You stroked my hair and sang me songs that spoke of taking every step forward with my hand in yours, for it will always be a step toward something bigger and better than where I currently am. When I walk through life holding your hand, I know that I am exactly where I am meant to be in any given moment, coupled with a strong sense of direction and an unwavering conviction that all is well in my world when you are in it.

I have used the power of your elevated frequency during my struggles, and within that space found previously unnoticed strengths. You have helped me create awareness within, of all that I already have, helping me grow and expand even more. As I have embodied your commandment, your description of a successful mode of living, doing, and being; my thankful heart has opened my eyes to the multitude of blessings that continually surround me.

I still remember the days before I connected intimately with you. I knew about you, but never fully comprehended your ability to totally transform lives. I always knew I wanted to get to know you more but waited for an invitation to be part of your inner circle, never knowing that an open invitation was always there.

Initially, to gain access to you and get closer to you, I have to admit that I used my friend Joy to make it into your inner circle. Joy was a simple form of gratitude. Joy definitely helped me grow and expand by bringing in even more Joy and Laughter into my life. But I knew in my heart that I needed just a little bit more, and of course, I was ready for more.

I recall Thankfulness introducing me directly to you in the end, and that was the beginning of a beautiful relationship with you. My relationship with Thankfulness was wonderful, too, but mainly consisted merely of words. As my relationship with you has developed and deepened over time, I got to understand that Gratitude is the completion of Thankfulness and is shown in acts, not thoughts alone. I finally got it. The penny dropped.

Your consistent daily reminders at first, to train myself to never put off a word or action for the expression of gratitude, was a tremendously useful starting point, grounding me solidly in my relationship with you. Over time, the reminders have become no longer necessary as the practice is embodied. Making you my daily expression, I have come to know right to the core of my entire being that the highest appreciation is not simply to utter the words but rather to live by them. Thank you. This has been life altering in terms of direction and trajectory.

The more my relationship with you developed, the more I realised, Gratitude, that you are both a choice and a mindset. Initially, one may choose to practice the thought or act of gratitude, but with time it becomes embedded and becomes the mindset. A thankful thought is truly the highest form of thought that exists. Not confined to the head but travelling to the heart space, too.

I have replaced my friend Complaining with you, beloved Gratitude...

Being grateful for what I have stopped me from hanging out with Complaining. Complaining had an uncanny knack of boring everyone else. She did nothing to solve any of my problems and therefore did me no good. Complaining was rather like a virus; she unwittingly created ripples of a lower frequencies that were then shared unconsciously with others; and it then grew.

Life is a continuous circle of giving and receiving energy.

I have witnessed that being thankful for who and what is in my life, instead of complaining about what I don't have, has opened me up to attracting prosperity and abundance. Gratitude, you shift everything. You are the type of energy that shifts shit.

Gratitude, I find myself trying to define you further.

Today, sitting in my gratitude garden surrounded by the song of sparrows, I breathe in gratitude and feel its full expression as *happiness doubled by wonder*. Happiness cannot be travelled to... owned, earned, won, or consumed. Happiness: the spiritual experience of living every minute with love, grace, and gratitude.

If I wanted to find happiness, I needed to find you... my darling Gratitude! You have been my prerequisite to happiness. When I came to recognise that what I already have is enough, it became more than enough, and I uncannily opened myself up to more.

The more grateful I am, the more beauty I see. It would be true to say that my struggles end where my gratitude begins, and boy-oh-boy there is ALWAYS *something* to be grateful for, which undoubtedly turns what I have into enough and more. I chuckle reading this last sentence that I have written to you, for I can see how long I was blind before sharing my life with you. You have created within me the capacity to see the pattern within the pattern. The more I use your presence in my life, the more fulfilling presence in my life I gain. Being fully present, grounded in the moment with gratitude, means that all fears from the past slip away and all anxieties for the future are erased because both fear and anxiety cannot co-exist in your sunny presence. They melt like soft-serve ice cream on a hot summer's day.

The things I take for granted each day are some of the very things that most deserve my gratitude, and as I strengthen my relationship with you, I have noticed that niggly fears start to disappear and abundance appears, unlocking the fullness of life. You shift me to a higher frequency where I can attract and call in much better things.

Oh, Gratitude, you have the uncanny magical ability to turn denial into acceptance, chaos to order, and confusion to clarity. When you entered my life and became the essential foundation upon which I built my life, miracles started to appear everywhere. This powerful process of shifting my energy brought MORE of what I WANTED into my life. As I started to be grateful for what I already had, the more I attracted in good things, and with that the tide of disappointment went out and the tide of love rushed in.

You, Gratitude, are the sweetest thing in a seeker's life; in fact, to border on boldness, I would say all human life, for when we have you in our heart there is a tremendous sweetness in our eyes and a kinder lens through which we view our world, with which we go on to treat our world.

I find that you are stored best in my heart and not just my mind. From within this thankful heart of mine, my eyes are opened to the multitude of blessings that continually surround us all. It is true! The more grateful I am, the more beauty there is to see, and what a wonderful cycle it is to be circulating in.

And then I bear witness to your effect within others and see there is nothing more honourable than their grateful heart, their gratitude, a sign of a noble soul. When others show up in my life with you, Gratitude, it is quite possibly the simplest yet most powerful thing one human can do for another. There is nothing more beautiful than when you feel your own light going out and it is rekindled by the spark of another person with their frequency of gratitude. Their gratitude can transform a garden-variety day into an elevated day of thanksgiving. In their giving of Gratitude, we are received.

And yet it is in our giving of Gratitude that we receive, too.

When valuing life, appreciating the hidden blessings, acknowledging the aspects of good that I already have, contemplating how amazing the elements of life are, I consistently build a strong foundation for abundance. Even being thankful for struggles, which sounds insanely counter-intuitive, I have indeed discovered my strengths. It's an extraordinary gift. You gave me everything without asking for anything in return. You changed my world, and I can't (or choose not to) imagine what it would be like if I hadn't met you.

You alone have managed to permanently erase the concept of my life being a nightmare at times and exchanged it for a reality where my life is filled with dreams that come true as I speak them into being.

I think with deep gratitude for those have lit the flame within me with their gratitude, as it is a powerful catalyst for happiness, a spark that lights a fire of joy within my soul.

Gratitude, you are indeed the charming gardener who makes our souls blossom, and I am grateful to you for making me happy. Practicing Gratitude truly is the fairest blossom that springs from the soul. Upon waking each morning, before opening my eyes, with a pressing urgency I think of only three of the most important things:

Thank you.
Thank you.
Thank you.
I start each and every day with you, Gratitude.

And as I lay my head to rest at the end of the day, I close my day off with three thoughts:

Thank you.
Thank you.
Thank you.
I end each and every day with you, Gratitude.

Thankful. Grateful. Blessed.

Your life-long, adoring companion,

Taryn Claire

Chapter 8

Patricia Diano

The steering wheel was yanked to the left, the car spinning around and around so many times that the streetlights flashed like a disco. The tree trunk was vivid, so close to my face that I remember thinking, Is *this it? Is my life over?* just as the car came to a screeching halt, parking itself in front of two poles and jarring the door so I was unable to open it.

What the f#!k just happened? My heart racing a million miles an hour, I was speechless at such a ruthless act from another human. I didn't know what to feel – anger, frustration, sheer disappointment? I looked over to the 'ex' on the passenger side, not knowing whether to punch him in the face or cry.

I was in such shock that I made it mean it was my fault and refused help from the kind people that stopped.

I was 19 or 20 years at the time, with unhealthy levels of self-esteem, self-doubt, self-confidence – all the "selfs" that the majority, if not all, of us experience at some point in our lives. Staying in a toxic, damaging relationship was easier than trusting my intuition and getting the hell outta there.

The sheer fear of thinking about the latter would keep me in this relationship for six years. What on earth made me stay? I knew, two years before I left him, what I needed to do, but at the time, remaining the same was a lot easier than deciding to make a change. Can you relate?

Change was the most difficult thing I had to do. It was like the old me had to die first to make room for the new. If only someone would have shown me a simple way to curl up and die, to then re-emerge as a beautiful butterfly, now that would have made my journey so much easier.

I made the decision to change and to be *truly grateful for the whole kit and caboodle.* There were many times where I handled situations and events in, let's just say, very unresourceful ways. I definitely handled challenges and dealt with them badly, which consequently led me to react instead of rationally responding. Let's talk more on this in a moment.

Now I find solitude in journaling and using the many tools I learnt and created along my journey, which allow me to see and be thankful for *every single thing*, even when situations are not working to plan. It's not easy to understand why things are not working to plan, but it's simple once you know how.

Be the Change and Get What You Want

The pitter patter of footsteps came racing down the corridor, into our room, and those 8-year-old little feet jumped into our bed and proclaimed, "Oh, Mamma, I have a sore throat, I can't go to school today."

Oh no, I thought, he has Mondayitis. Here we go. Little did he know I was very experienced in this field. In year nine, I had a sore throat seven times in a 14-week span.

As I placed his lemon and honey tea on the bedside table, we shared a moment. He thought he had it in the bag. He rolled over, and as he did I gently whispered, "That's okay, my baby, you can get better today by staying in bed all day with no tv or devices, and I'll let your cousins know they can't come for a sleep over because you're sick."

Kiss kiss and I left.

Oh wow, I have never seen anyone become so well in such a short time. Truly a delight to watch his little face tell me he was feeling better. I was certainly bursting on the inside – so cute.

At that moment, I realised change was sooo crucial for success. Most humans 'think' too much, instead of 'feeling' their way through life. My little one's connection with his cousins was the driver to feeling better than 'thinking' about not going to school.

I was thinking too much about what 'might' happen if I left him instead of trusting my feeling about the relationship. I was too caught up in his journey, instead of trusting my intuition and flying free with what I knew I needed to do.

I remember, watching the movie *The Secret*, how pumped I was. I wondered in awe: *All I have to do is think about what I want, and then it magically appears!* Can that be right? Well, yes, it is partly correct. They just forgot to mention the part about matching up to the *feeling of having* it even before it is physically yours. Then, and only then, does the magic happen. It is the foundation of manifesting your every desires. Beliefs, or your manifested desires, are active vibrations that resonate through you to attract more of that which is you. I'm really excited to be sharing more on this a bit later.

Changing how I viewed the world was the first step to my success. I must admit, my first few attempts were clunky. My husband Peter and I were home one evening when I decided to share my idea. I think I can, I think I can, so I leaped and fell splat on my face. I'm still laughing just thinking about it.

"Honey, I'm learning to meditate," I said, my chest inflated as I stood in my Wonder Woman pose and total confidence. That didn't last long. I'm sure the entire suburb heard him laughing. He knew I couldn't sit still for more than a minute. I had to agree, *This is gonna take some work,* giggling to myself. I'll talk about how I achieved that shortly.

My big revelation came when I realised we live in a feeling world; we must feel our way through in order to get what we want. That's the simplest way I can describe it.

How you feel *has* to match what you think in order to match up to what you want. If you are just thinking your way through, you'll be waiting a while.

As Joe Dispenza explains, 95% of our actions are unconscious. This 95% is ruled by the part of the brain that has an important role to keep us safe and rarely likes change. This is also known as our default system or our ego. All of this learnt unconscious behaviour was cemented between the ages 0 and 7 years of age. So essentially, I believe, most humans are allowing their 0–7-years-olds run their lives as a mature adult. Dealing with problems, communicating with people, and the everyday stresses of life are dealt with as a child.

My Italian heritage means my learnt behaviour of having a conversation is yelling, and how funny it is to watch my 10-year-old, Massimo, and 8-year-old, Alessandro, do the same when Nonno is around.

Our brain is plastic, which means it is mouldable. So, training our brain, being conscious of our thoughts and grateful of what is and was, is the way to match up to what we want.

You *can* change. You just have to believe you can.

React or Respond: You Decide

Emotional intelligence (EI), in my opinion, is more important than intelligence quotient (IQ). As humans, we are controlled by our emotions. Our emotions depict the way we feel and how we react to situations.

"Eat your breakfast, boys. Please eat your breakfast. Come on, boys, it's been 20 minutes and you're still sitting there, eat your breakfast."

Sound familiar? Whether you're a parent or a child, we all know what happens next, right? Okay, I confess, it was me. I lost my shit. I felt all my blood rush to my head. Need I say more? Clearly, my default system took over.

The simplest and easiest way I dealt with challenges was to react to them, as it allowed me to be significant, even if it was just for a moment. It allowed me to get someone's attention, which really was a cry for love. *Somebody love me, please.*

Reacting to a situation is merely someone triggering something within us that we have not dealt with, either as a child or to a situation that triggers an emotion linked to that situation. So, the boys being told over and over again to finish their breakfast triggered me because I felt no one was listening. A deep trauma in my early childhood where I not felt heard surfaced and I lost my cool. At the time, blaming them for my reaction was stopping my growth, stopping me from being a better wife, mother, daughter, and friend. I handed my power to another because I did not take responsibility for my own actions. I am the only person that can change me.

I love the breathing technique to re-balance my body. It helps me calm my sympathetic nervous system, which is our fight, flight, or freeze response to stressful situations. I was diagnosed with chronic fatigue, and this was an important part of my journey. My tiredness was persistent, and I did what I needed to do to balance myself, naturally. Breathing was one of those tools in my kit. It is certainly underestimated, and I highly recommend to all.

Another tool I use in these situations that keeps me being mindful is taking five minutes to check in with myself and ask, "Who am I being right now? How is this serving me? And what can I do better?"

Now that I am consciously aware of my emotions, I allow myself to stop. Adjust my tone, posture, choice of words, and pitch. Tony Robbins refers to it as "changing your state".

I want to be in my parasympathetic nervous system, which helps me connect back to my relaxed state, as soon as possible and as often as possible.

The parasympathetic, aka 'rest and digest', also helps stimulate our digestion and activate our metabolism, so imagine what happens to us when we are constantly stressed or worried.

Do 'the Work'

"Honey, I'm learning to meditate."

Not quite the reaction I expected; however, it was definitely warranted at the time. I could not sit still if my life depended on it. Too much going on upstairs hindered my ability to succeed in the way I wanted, AND I could not understand why.

Quite often I'd listen to inspirational and motivational speakers; I had my business mentors plus listen to podcasts, and one of their secrets would lead to doing 'the Work'. What on earth were they talking about was the question in my mind. What work?

'The Work', might I add, took me places I never thought possible, and I am still climbing. Turning in the direction of wellbeing was the best thing since sliced bread for me. I am forever grateful for my life experiences and what I have learnt so far. It changed my marriage, the way I parent, and, most importantly, the way I felt about myself.

Okay, meditation time. I was so eager to get started, like a little girl going on a shopping spree, jittery but with big smiles. I was sitting on my special chair with my eyes closed. I had my music playing, lit some colourful candles, and took my first strategic meditation lesson. Ha, who was I kidding! Quieting my mind was far from fun. Buzz, buzz, buzz was all that was churning for the entire two minutes I attempted to meditate. Thoughts flying around everywhere – it's simply impossible to stop thinking. I'd have to die to stop thinking.

We all have to start somewhere, right, and I can thankfully say that with consistency, commitment, and practice I did it. I now proudly mediate for a minimum of 15 minutes per day. Have no fear: here are the steps.

Step One

Before you start, get yourself in a state of thinking about pleasant things. Even if you have a favourite mantra, say that 15 times. The morning is the best time as the mind is still in hypnosis.

Step Two

Make sure you are comfortable. Wear loose clothing, dim the lights, or use no lights, sit in a comfy chair. Whatever it is for you that gets you relaxed. Hey, stay awake, though.

Step Three

Focus your attention on a noise that is consistent, like the split system or even the ringing in your own ears. Just make sure it is constant and consistent.

Step Four

Breathe gently. There are going to be times when your mind will start to wander, especially when you first start. That's all good. Just be aware and gently invite your mind back, thank it, and focus your attention on that noise again.

Step Five

Relax. Allow your body to feel the shift, feel the tingles, feel the lightness, feel the expansion. Welcome to your higher self!!!

My real break-though was when I started journaling after my meditations. After meditating, I was in a higher vibration. This meant I was able to tune in and listen better. Understanding the implications of our vibrational frequency helped me become a better version of myself.

To understand vibrational frequency, we must understand our entire universe is energy. Energy has a frequency or a vibration. This vibration is what makes water water, humans humans, and so on. An atom, which is essentially what we are all made from, presents itself as a solid, liquid, or gas. An atom is energy.

Everything has a frequency/vibration. That frequency allows us to see, feel, hear, touch, and smell.

For example, a flower is a flower because its vibrational frequency is that which makes it a flower, and it knows exactly how to be a flower by how it was energetically and genetically made.

A great way to understand this is in our understanding of the radio. We know, to hear Fox FM, we need to dial it to 101.9 FM. If it's on any other number, we won't be on the same frequency, so we're unable to hear it.

This is the same for our human frequency or vibration. When we are living in the vibrations of anger, all we see is anger. When we are set on joy, all we see is joy. Do you think we are going to hear anyone joyful when all we feel is anger? Absolutely not.

When we are sending our frequencies out into the world, we are going to find situations that MATCH our frequency. We will hear, smell, taste, touch everything around us that MATCHES us. When we are angry, we are going to see only anger around us. When we have no money, we are only going to attract more of the same thing, a lack of or no money.

"Why the hell does this sh*t keep happening?"

I felt goosepimples run all the way up the back of my neck, my cheeks heating up and my nostrils flaring. My pay cheque was spent before it was earnt. I had three jobs and still struggled with money. It was a downward spiral and made no sense to me at the time. I was earning an apprentice hairdresser wage, worked at a charcoal chicken shop, and on the weekends had a waitressing job – and still could not manage. You know the saying, "When it rains it pours"? I smashed my car three times in a six-week span, supported my ex financially, and felt like I was going nowhere, fast.

I was stuck in low vibration frequencies for a really long time. My plans would fall flat, and it felt like life would never change. My vibration was in such "victim mode" that I could not hear and comprehend when someone was helping me or communicating kindness.

True gratitude came when I understood and took full responsibility for myself and my actions. The good, the bad, and the ugly – it was all me. What I had in my life, *I attracted*. Yes, even the bad stuff.

I certainly manifested the correct people at the correct time on my journey to healing, and recognising that I was fully responsible was a game changer. How I felt and what I thought shaped my experiences and gave me more of those experiences by my point of attraction. My gratitude journaling, without a doubt, was my saviour for success.

Die to Live

My life map – the stories I told myself based on my understanding of the world through experiences, relationships, values and beliefs, role models, understanding the world and perceptions of my environment – equalled my reality.

I had to unlearn my 0–7-year-old reality and relearn it by changing my behaviours, habits, and patterns. The reality I had served me well until it didn't. Until I made the decision to change because my reality basically sucked.

Releasing my old self gave me the strength and courage to be the best role model for my family and, ultimately, for myself.

Journaling, breathing, staying curious, being consciously aware, and many more tools helped me through my life's obstacles. I sincerely hope it does the same for you as my next chapter shares my gratitude journal technique that you can begin to use now. Blessing and love.

My Gratitude Journal

The power of writing has saved my sanity and pushed me to new highs I never thought possible. Feeling gratitude every day lifts my spirits and allows me to connect to Infinite Source and have better relationships, with myself and others.

My intention for you is to feel the best you have ever felt because you have committed to you! Deliberate self-suggestions, deliberate manifesting, deliberate creating and co-creating at its best.

My journal is to be used as a place for you to dream big, to really feel the feelings of what you want as if you already have them and be grateful for having them. This is the most important secret. *You have to imagine as if you already have it.* Remember, what you think about, you become about. Really feel it, get excited, imagine it in your mind's eye as if it is already yours, get creative, and get in the picture. Make it real. What do you see, feel, hear, smell, taste, touch? Your brain does not know the difference between real and imagined, so imagine it into reality. Imagine BIG. More that you could ever dream of.

This simple practice is immensely powerful. We can be so caught up in the busyness of life. Embracing and stepping into gratitude allows us to tap into the joy and wonder and really have fun in the unfolding of our lives.

Remember to be gentle with your self during this process, as change does not happen overnight. It is a gradual happening, so enjoy the ride!

Chapter 9

Dr Carolyn Smith-Keune

Rediscovering gratitude at sea

Introduction

I have always lived an adventurous life. I was born with the spirit of exploration in my veins and a natural curiosity that bubbles out of me. I have a deep fondness for learning about different cultures and deep respect for all of life's varied and wonderful creatures. I enjoyed more than two decades as a marine scientist before becoming the manager of a busy and exciting genetics research laboratory. I am now attempting a career change, starting my own mental health advocacy and wellness company, Wellness Warriors United Pty Limited.

I am an eternal optimist who wears rose-colored glasses deliberately and with pride. I have always looked for the best in myself, and in others. Now in mid-life, I continue to grow this skill. I joyously undertake my own unique "Heroines Healing Journey". I am learning to slow down and am taking a break from science to "do the work" of healing from burnout and rebounding from life-altering mental health issues.

Among my many grand life adventures, I experienced some significant challenges. A "Trifecta of Trauma" molded me into a strong, fiercely independent but also highly nurturing person. Instrumental in my healing has been counting my many blessings and expressing my gratitude for them daily. I am grateful even for the difficult life lessons the tough times have taught me. Adventure and adversity have made me a more well-rounded, wiser, and grounded woman and have resulted in a kind, caring, compassionate, and heart-centered mother, daughter, sister, and friend. Here is just one of the unique life stories for which I am eternally grateful. Enjoy.

A Gem of a Reef

The 19th of October 2021 was when I took back agency over my life and began filling my bucket first. I had been burning the candle at both ends, caring for everyone except myself. In early 2018 I burnt out and struggled to shake off debilitating chronic migraines for nearly four years. The extreme dizziness of these "vestibular" migraines robbed me of my ability to function at home and work. Eventually, I lost hope that anything could be done, as one drug after another failed to control the daily migraines. I was spending days and weeks in a darkened bedroom with little meaningful interaction with my family and friends. Depression soon set in, and I became highly anxious when at work. My usually optimistic outlook disappeared, and I began to focus on what I couldn't do rather than on what I could. My family and I were stuck in no man's land, just existing. Thankfully, all that changed following five weeks of "Mindfulness at Work" training, during which I met and employed a life coach. It was the best investment in myself I could have made. By October 2021, my coach had helped me to discover the healing power of daily gratitude and the vital importance of filling my cup. I desperately wanted to be a good role model to my teenage daughter. I wanted her to see me leading a truly fulfilling life by following my passions and doing what I love. I wanted to inspire her and show her the path to being her best self in all her relationships.

Our daughter's birth was the most magical day of my life. Looking down into her beautiful blue eyes, so full of love and trust, I forgot how heartbroken I had been when my first pregnancy ended in miscarriage. Anxiety was replaced with excitement when at last my pregnant belly swelled to make room for the girl that I hoped might one day want to be my dive buddy. Unexpectedly, not long after I first felt her kick, severe pelvic pain kicked in. From 20 weeks onwards, SPD (symphysis pubis dysfunction) impeded my mobility and disrupted sleep. It was made bearable by my already fierce and protective maternal love for our rapidly growing daughter. I knew she was a fighter from the moment I heard her heartbeat on the ultrasound, and we were all soon glad of her fighting spirit. My heart stopped as the nurse wheeled our 12-hour-old bundle of joy away from me to the neo-natal ward, suspicious that she had a potentially deadly 'superbug' infection. The challenges to her young life were not over when we took her home. I watched on in horror as she gagged, choked, and broke out in hives while drinking her first bottle of formula at 8 months old. We soon learned our colicky and eczema-covered baby had life-threatening allergies to milk, eggs, and possibly other things. Keeping our daughter healthy, safe, and well become my highest priority. I willingly changed my career direction to make sure I was there for her, and as a result, I stopped SCUBA diving.

I had been a SCUBA diver since the age of 15 and I had loved diving with my mum, dad, and brother in the Northern Territory before going to university in Queensland. Once there, I dived regularly with colleagues and co-workers on the Great Barrier Reef, living out my dream career as a marine biologist. Being out at sea for weeks and working 45 minutes out of town at the Australian Institute of Marine Science (AIMS) didn't feel "safe" for me once our highly allergic daughter came along. I wanted to be close to the daycare and schools (in case of allergic reactions). I also desired job stability, so I changed my research focus from coral biology to aquaculture genetics, where jobs were available in Townsville close to home. I could have joined a dive club, but diving on the reef is a rather expensive hobby, so as the lone SCUBA diver in the family I chose to spend my weekends with them and focus during the week on the challenging juggle of being a working mother and being present as a wife. Interestingly, as our daughter grew out of her allergies and entered the more independent teenage years, I replaced caring for her with excessively caring for my workmates. At least until I physically and mentally burnt out and started going through what I now call the

"Great Unraveling", or "the breakdown I had to have".

With my health in tatters, and the words of my life coach ringing in my ear, I knew it was time to take care of myself and break the diving drought. I decided to go to my coach's "Soul Compass" weekend retreat in Port Douglas, and I added on a solo diving holiday. I was confident I would find a dive buddy on a tourist boat or be able to dive with one of the onboard dive masters. So, I packed a tent in my car and headed north to where the reef is closest to the coast, leaving "the teenager" at home with her very capable father. On that gloriously sunny day in October, I stood alone on the dock looking up at *Calypso*, the sleek blue catamaran that would take me out to the reef that day. The butterflies in my tummy fluttered, tickling my insides in a delightful dance of anticipation. Fifteen years. It had been 15 years since I had dived the Great Barrier Reef, or anywhere for that matter. I was anxious to see what state the reefs were in.

The *Calypso* crew greeted me cheerily and introduced me to Pamela, the lovely dive master, who looked at my completed onboarding forms and asked," Why has it been so long since your last dive?" She was flicking through my dive logs when I stated simply, "My daughter just turned 14". It was the simplest answer I could give, but it got me thinking as the boat quietly slipped out of the Port Douglas Marina and glided smoothly over piercing blue seas as calm as a pane of glass. When and where was my last dive? I pored over my dive log to find out.

My last recorded dive was for my old co-worker, Ray Berkelmans, a wonderful coral biologist and my regular dive buddy for more than four years. Ray and I were both studying coral bleaching, from our own unique and different perspectives, and I always enjoyed diving with him. During my PhD research we called our days on the water together our "mental health" days. Feeling miserable in the weeks after my miscarriage, and much in need of a mental health day, Ray kindly took me out for a day of diving as his volunteer. At the end of the day, Ray remembered he had yet to retrieve a temperature data logger from Middle Reef within the shallow bay of Townsville. By that time the sun was low in the sky, and the wind had picked up stirring the sediment and obscuring visibility. The boat heaved uncomfortably in the swell, so we agreed only two of us would dive. Ray's co-worker Damien and I both bravely volunteered. I watched on anxiously as Damien jumped in first, descending fast to avoid the propellors of the dangerously pitching boat. I took a deep and calming breath before I took my own giant stride into the murky water, immediately following Damien's bubbles down. I couldn't see him in the murk, and I was distracted by a school of large fish that appeared as eerie shadows around my head. I didn't know what hit me when Damien collided with me on his way up with the retrieved data logger already in his hand. I nearly had a heart attack, this being crocodile and shark territory, after all. It was the only time I was ever thankful to be out of the water in under 5 minutes! As the sun set over Townsville, we made our way back into port and I thanked Ray and told him just how grateful I was for the days diving, not knowing then how long it would be before I went again.

That mental health day out diving with Ray and Damien had shown me that I can always find some inner peace underwater, even when the conditions are not great, and I am grieving a tragic loss. Under the sea is clearly my happy place, and it was just what I needed to distract me from my grief at that time. Fifteen years later, as I steamed towards Opal Reef with the sea air blowing in my face aboard *Calypso*, I realized that not only was I in recovery from burnout, but I still carried a lot of unprocessed grief and trauma in my body, mind, and soul. It felt like years since I had taken a full, deep, and calming breath. On top of that, motherhood had been so life-altering that, like many mothers, I had woken up one day with a teenager and found myself looking at a stranger reflected in the mirror. "Who am I when I am not being a mother or a wife?" I asked my reflection. As Opal Reef appeared on the blue horizon, I heard a whisper from my old self. "You are a diver and a biologist", it said. It dawned on me that I was grieving at some deeper level the other things that I had lost or let go of: my coral biology career, carefree lazy weekends, and a slimmer, more youthful body. The wetsuit I pulled on in preparation for my dive was now tighter than I recalled it being, and I was traveling alone. I was mourning for the friendships that didn't survive the busyness of motherhood, and I longed to reconnect with like-minded friends and to reengage in other joyful hobbies I had left behind.

As we approached the reef, my tummy butterflies danced a little with just a touch of anxiety on top of the excitement. Alone onboard *Calypso*, I looked around and smiled at other happy tourists with their families or their friends, and I chatted to the crew, who were still strangers to me then. I had not dived in unfamiliar dive gear before, nor dived with a stranger in all my years of diving. Truthfully, it had taken a lot of courage to pack up a tent and camp as a solo 47-year-old woman on my way up to Port Douglas. I was proud of myself, and I was feeling empowered by the whole experience. I was grateful to have conquered the limiting belief that I couldn't do these things on my own. As it turned out, the dive master on board the *Calypso* was so warm and welcoming that I soon forgot that I was traveling alone. Pamela was rostered to take out the introductory divers and, although I was hardly a novice, the crew had expressed unease at the length of time since my last dive. To reassure them I agreed to dive with Pam and the 'intro' divers who were experiencing their first SCUBA dive. I found myself sitting patiently through "dive training" on the way out to the reef, and I watched with amusement as the effervescent Pam made the standard PADI dive material come to life with her hand gestures and exotic accent. It was like watching a puppet master enthralling the crowd at a show. Pam had everyone's rapt attention and she gave her spiel like a pro, which was as informative as it was entertaining. I was grateful for the crew's initial "unease", as it meant I got to dive with someone as reassuring and competent as Pam.

I even forgot to be self-conscious as I slipped into my now snug 1mm lycra "wetsuit". Thank goodness the zip did up and the seams stayed intact, I thought as I awkwardly pulled it on. I watched eagerly as the reef became clearly visible through my polaroid sunglasses. As *Calypso* pulled into the first of three dive sites, I could already tell that Opal Reef was a true gem. When the skipper finally hooked up to the mooring and I saw the reef close up, in all its glory, it took my breath away. Standing on the deck, I counted the black and tan sea cumbers cleaning up the sandy bottom 20 meters down below. I had forgotten how brilliantly clear the visibility is on the Northern Great Barrier

Reef. I visited similar outer-shelf reefs as a volunteer during my undergraduate days. I helped researchers measure the drop-off in agricultural and urban run-off in the north, and on the outer-shelf reefs along the edge of the continental shelf. It was one of the reasons I had made the trek from Townsville to Port Douglas for my first dive back after so many years. I was desperate for a good experience, and Opal Reef is bathed in the cool, clear waters welling up from the continental shelf. As we closed in on it, the sight of crystal-clear blue waters and gently breaking waves along the reef brought back so many spectacular carefree memories.

The crew tied up the *Calypso* with brisk efficiency. Before I knew it, I had my unfamiliar dive gear checked and donned, and I shuffled forward eagerly to take my giant stride. The back of *Calypso* was crowded with enthusiastic snorkelers, swimmers, and divers, but the crew directed us all with practiced cheer. I had to wait my turn on the surface of the water for the brief safety checks the intro divers must do before they descend. I waited patiently while I hung there in the open-water, marveling at the seascape that revealed itself below. I delighted at the fish that peeked cheekily out from underneath the boat and waved back happily at them. I laughed at the tenacity of the fish that bravely pecked at unsuspected divers when their backs were turned. I smiled broadly at Pam, who was putting us through our paces, and she beamed with delight back at me. It was, I think, a rare treat for her to be getting an experienced diver such as me back in the water, and she quickly realized just how special the day was to me.

We descended slowly, and Pam's pace was nice and sedate. She knew this patch of reef intimately and her love for it was clear. She waved to her friend the clownfish; she pointed out the tiny pipe-fish, with their black and white stripes, hiding under a ledge. She had told us she would find them, and she did. Pam knew all the good hiding places, and her repertoire of underwater hand signals was impressive, to say the least. Pam and I literally 'talked' with our hands underwater, playing a game of marine charades for the other divers. Pam was quite delighted that I was adept at finding cool critters and was willingly pointing them out to her and the others, too. Being a shark-nut herself, she was thrilled when I pointed out an epaulet shark hiding in the reef scape. That find earned me "many thanks" and "much love" in signal form!

Pam had dived on Opal more than a hundred times as a long-term crew member on the *Calypso*. When we first met, she told me I was going to love it, but I was not expecting what we found. I was blown away from the very first deep and healing breath beneath the surface. I had watched my local reefs turn white, and many corals die, during a heat wave in 2002. I knew the situation for many reefs had only gotten more dire since, and my expectations, I'll admit, were low. My relief at seeing such a vibrant, lively reef, full of marine life of every conceivable kind, was genuine and deep. I was wowed at first by a mass of deep purple and yellow ascidians (sea squirts), their open funnels barbed to stop the fish from swimming in. I had never seen so many all at once, not in all the 275 dives I had already done. My heart grew two sizes as I gazed in wonder, and relief, at the fields of big and small Porites coral bommies that we swam around. The colorful feather worms that inhabit them, in hues of red, orange, and bright blue, retreated rapidly as our shadow was cast upon them. Giant clams soaked up the sunshine and squirted us with water as they closed up when we swam above. Inch-long nudibranchs, gorgeous flatworms with feathered gills, stood out, their black, white, and yellow patterns contrasting against the abundant and healthy coral colonies they nestled on, and that we carefully swam around.

As a coral biologist of sorts, my sheer delight, and hope for the future grew with every tiny coral recruit I found. The newly budded polyps of baby corals waved at me from amongst their older peers, their rapidly growing tips glowing with brilliant pastel pinks, greens, and blues. I was ecstatic to see amongst them my favorite coral species, *Acropora millepora*, which I had studied for my PhD. Other corals I had thought were likely gone from the reef for good (*Pocillipora damicornis, Stylophora pistillata,* and *Seriata hysterix*) were also to be found in abundance. The sight of so many of them dulled my sadness at having watched these species disappearing further south on the inshore reefs. I was overjoyed to have found once again the incredibly clever and very cute commensal crabs nestled safely in the delicate branches of a *Seriata hysterix* colony. The tiny crab had tricked the thin and pointy branches of the coral into growing towards each other and broadening out like two open hands, complete with several little fingers, clasped loosely together. It was the perfect, safe, and secure home for the crab and a very welcome sign of a healthy, diverse, and fully functioning reef ecosystem. I was grateful for the sight of it. Tiny colorful coral gobies (small, bluish-green inch-long commensal fish) also peeked out at me from their host coral colonies, and their presence cemented my relief.

I couldn't help but smile, too, when I lay back and looked across the reef at the dashing, dancing clouds of fish around it that affirmed the vigor of Opal Reef. Later in the day, on my last of three dives, I was treated to the sight of a large school of sweetlips spawning above the reef. The dull females raced upwards with bright red males dashing after in hot pursuit. The clouds of fish spawn they left in the water were a wonderful and promising sign of good fishing days ahead. No dive for me is ever quite complete until I spy a *Moorish Idol*, though. Opal Reef did not disappoint. On all three dives, I caught sight of Idols flitting over the substrate. In one case, three of them passed me by as I watched with some amusement the open-mouthed coral trout get a dental clean at the local 'cleaning station'. A hardworking little blue and black striped cleaner fish picked parasites diligently off the happy coral trout. The royal-looking white, black, and yellow Moorish Idols, with their long, trailing upper fin, were a reassuring sign to me. These intriguing fish are emblematic of and closely associated with fond memories of my early diving days. I think I was fascinated by them because I couldn't work out what they ate. I thought their long, slender beaks must be for eating corals, just like the abundant and colorful butterfly fish. Happy memories flooded back too when I spied three 'teenage' batfish hovering, as delicate as gently swaying seaweed strands; they stayed tucked up safely inside a cavern at the edge of the reef. Surrounding them, a massive school of see-through glass fish ebbed and flowed with the gently rocking sea. They parted to let the batfish through, and I couldn't hold back my grin. I signaled my love to Pam with gloved hands and she grinned back at me, thanking me for the share.

My dive log reads "Absolutely bloody spectacular, the reef is glowing with vitality" and, for my final dive that day, "Ripper of a dive". Every entry from that day ended with either "lovely" or "I loved it!" By the time my waterlogged body emerged for the final time that day, Pam and I were firm friends. We had bonded through our sheer and continual delight at all the critters we had seen. Pam had shared with me her names for her regulars, the fish that is. I had watched with both understanding and amusement as she had a chat with a clownfish she clearly knew quite well. As the day wound to a close, I came to appreciate Pam's incredible skill and admired her patience in taking complete novices down onto the reef. Everyone I watched go into the water nervous, came out with smiles from ear to ear. The depth of my gratitude for the kindness of Pam and the *Calypso* crew cannot be overstated. I determined then and there that I would bring my family back and take them for an 'intro' dive with Pam and me. I have since done exactly that, and it was just as marvelous. I now return there every three or four months and ask for Pam, and if she is rostered on, she kindly asks the skipper to take me somewhere new. I have plans to return for my 300th dive in early 2023.

I am eternally grateful that the visit to Opal Reef not only brought back my passion for diving but also brought me closer to my loved ones. I have now had two dives with my daughter, and she is enthusiastic to become my future dive buddy. I am so proud of her for overcoming anxiety and jumping in the water bravely, and so thankful she got to see the Great Barrier Reef at its finest. Her confidence on her second dive was fantastic, and seeing her floating peacefully and calmly above the reef, even when a reef shark made an appearance, made my heart sing. Discovering a thriving healthy reef and being able to share that with my daughter brings great joy and gratitude to my life.

I have since been blessed with the opportunity to take my parents out on *Calypso* also. Watching my dad holding my daughter's hand underwater, much as he once held mine, was a heartwarming experience. Being able to hold my own mother's hand when she got back in the water too was a very special moment. The trip with my parents, now in their seventies, filled me with gratitude that will last a lifetime. It was their first dive in over 20 years, and possibly their last. What I am most grateful for, though, is that I have learned I am brave enough and happy to go out on a dive boat on my own. I am thankful that in middle age my confidence has grown, and I am proud that I am no longer limited by a perceived need to know my dive buddy or fear of traveling alone. Even now in my middle age, I feel safe, supported, held, and inspired underwater. Remembering what that felt like reminds me how much SCUBA diving fills my cup and brings out the best in me.

Finding happiness at the bottom of the sea again brings great inner peace and gratitude back into my life. I know now that there is truly nowhere but the reef that I would like to spend eternity, and I'll be back whenever I need to fill my bucket. If I had died on the way back from Opal Reef that day last October, I would have died happy and content. I am so grateful for the evolution coach who encouraged me to live my most fulfilling life and gave me the skills I needed to get myself out of the rut that I was in. Jody Michelle Perry, my evolution coach, taught me the power of gratitude. Making gratitude a regular morning practice has helped me find my way back to things I love. Gratitude practice has helped me see the beauty in the world again, even on the dark days when I am feeling down. Expressing gratitude for the things I get to do reminds me of what I CAN do and keeps me doing them. It helps me know when my bucket is getting low and when it is time for a refill. Gratitude is the medicine I needed to truly begin to heal. The rewards for my own physical and mental health have been enormous, and I will never stop expressing daily gratitude. This simple practice has had a profoundly positive impact on my relationships with those I love. The healing power of gratitude has helped me to align my body, mind, and soul, and it has given me back a life I love, and one that fulfills me every single day in some way.

I now express gratitude daily in my journal, starting with something small, something big, and something about myself. Diving Opal Reef was my something BIG on that day last October when I returned to SCUBA diving after 15 years away. I would be so honored to connect with you to share more stories like this one. I am delighted I can now share these powerful gratitude journaling tools in my Wellness Warriors United Gratitude Journal. I hope you will pick one up and join me on this grateful journey through our most fulfilled and fulfilling lives.

Chapter 10

Helen Cowley

Get up and dance. Your mind is a powerful thing.

When you fill your mind with gratitude, positive thoughts, and belief in the value of people, your life can change.

What you feel you attract. What you imagine you create. – Buddha

I was lying in bed feeling sorry for myself one morning. My little 3-year-old came to my bedside. I looked at him and immediately registered that he was all puffy. I could see he was sick and wanted to go to the toilet again for the tenth time. I dragged myself out of bed to take him to the bathroom, and I immediately noticed his urine was dark. Oh great! Another trip to the hospital!

I was the mother of five young children, all two years apart. I was struggling through another bout of depression. My mother had suffered from depression when I was a child, so I was determined not to go down the same path. Everyone has pressure and events in their life that can put them into that headspace that is just so hard to get out of. How we get out takes different paths; this was just my path, but one I share in the hope you will also find the strength and gratitude of your own mindset, determination, and friends.

My eldest had ADD. My husband was leaving at 5 am and getting home late every day. I felt my life wasn't worth much and was just there for everyone else. I was lonely and didn't want to get out of bed. So, most days, I would walk the children to the bus in my pyjamas, take the younger ones to day-care, and come home to go back to bed.

After realising my youngest had medical issues that required urgent and possibly prolonged attention, I decided that I just could no longer lie in bed all the time and feel sorry for myself – I had to get up, change myself – and look after my children. Of course, I had to make that change somehow. This wasn't easy, but it was the first essential step. There were many more steps and stages to come.

While the children were still young, our family business had been growing. My husband and I were running a fabrication and mobile repair business in Brisbane. This business was doing tender work for big fabrication projects for Fishermans Island and Stanwell Powerstation, employing 14–16 tradespeople, cost estimators, and admin staff. A recession and a project that was going to linger on for months meant having to negotiate with suppliers, creditors, and debtors. I was tired and overwhelmed. I had been managing my children and staff most days while my husband saw to the mobile earthmoving repair side of the business.

Each day would involve dropping one or two children at a day-care on the way to work and having a playroom and nursery for the others at work. Managing staff, project managing the contracts, looking after training and workplace issues, trying to understand drawings that would sometimes not be correct, and financial management. I would collect the children on the way home (40 minutes away) at about 4–5 pm. Get home, bathe the children, make dinner, and take dinner back to work for my husband, who would then review what we had achieved for the day, check the plans for the next stage, and help prepare for the next day before heading back home with sleepy children. Our lease had just come to a rollover, and we decided to get out and just work from home with the mobile service. Great, it would be easier! Or at least I thought so.

Managing a downsizing is different and difficult when you have ongoing contracts that should have finished but turned to extend another 12 months of deliveries and held-up payments, and, of course, negotiating with debtors and creditors to keep everyone happy and everyone paid on top of packing, transporting, and storing equipment and letting staff go.

As a mother, you can quite easily lose yourself to your children, your husband, or even to a degree – for me, it was my husband's business. I had nothing left of me – or so I thought. At the time, other businesses often asked me for help with planning and staffing issues. At first, I didn't understand that I was offering them value. I didn't BELIEVE I was skilled, as I was 'just a mother' helping her husband run the business. Eventually, this led me to start my own consulting business, but first, I had a lot of work to do on my mindset (beliefs) to even recognise the skill I had and the opportunity that was there.

During my time of negative mindset—depression, I had a friend who would come and talk to me, and he would encourage me to get out and go visit and help other people. "Come with me, take my hand." He continually encouraged me to come and help with St Vincent de Paul. To see how the other side lives. I didn't join St Vincent de Paul; however, I did get involved with social justice and helping the long-term unemployed through my church's social justice group. My faith has been one of those stables in my life and part of everything I do. Even in hard times, when you feel you are lonely or lost, it is there and not strong, but it comes back to stand by you just like a friend – like the footprints in the sand. The social justice project I was involved in for 12 years made me recognise there are those much worse off than me. So, starting to create gratitude for my own abilities – *by helping others, you help yourself* – you learn what you know and what you need to learn, and you can teach others. Funnily enough, there I started talking about our mindset and our mind chatter, goal setting, and believing in ourselves.

This was something that led to me understanding myself more. Helping others to set goals led me to write my own life mission statement. In wanting to teach others, I learned a process that took me through acknowledging my own strengths and interests. I managed to make it quite clear and focused. My life statement became:

To develop and broaden my education, experience, abilities, and skills in the area of related business, family, and government issues that affect the very small (micro) and family businesses – in order to benefit my family, my business, and the wider community.

This life statement was a bit wordy; however, it has stuck with me and reminded me of my life's direction in all the things I do. It also supports my belief about writing business plans and creating strategies, as I believe "the more focused a strategy, the easier it is to implement." And for me my statement has guided my education development and decisions for many years.

My friend who encouraged me to volunteer also encouraged me to go study. This was a big block for me as I did not BELIEVE (again) I could do it. I was not good at school. I had been told that I didn't have the ability to study and not to bother "because it was a waste of time and I was wasting my parents' money." Although I enjoyed school, my mother took me out during year 11 and told me to *find a man and get married.* It was this ingrained belief that I could not learn that I was fighting against as a 40-year-old adult.

We had one of our clients asking me again to help them, which again, I believed I couldn't do because I felt I was not qualified. Something finally clicked for me and I signed up for a TAFE course that I'd seen in the local paper. This was a BIG step towards expanding my mind and not allowing my previous beliefs to hold me back.

When I did take up a course in business, I was lucky enough to have a lecturer who again (took my hand) encouraged me to continue to university. Those relationships we have along the way are something to be grateful for... someone believing and helping to change my mindset! Our mindset can make or break our own development but also the relationship we have on the way to where we are going, when you start to have more of a positive mindset and can generally stay focused – that you have to be thankful that it changes your entire outcome and look at life and at friendships.

Here I was in my 40s, with five children who had not finished high school and husband who was not home till late. Not much money in the bank, and so again I developed strategies. I went to university during the day and studied at night. I focused on the things that mattered and made a difference to me and my thinking – I was able to overcome the negative thinking by different means, and I still use finding strategies and focus to gain my outcomes as a strength.

I'm truly grateful for the many strategies that keep my mind occupied and that have helped me achieve outcomes and brought me to the place I am today. The combination of my mindset strategies – focus and vision, my faith, my relationships, systems, and my learning – have brought me to a much brighter place in my life.

Our minds are one of our most important assets in life, and managing and controlling our mindset is not easy. And one of the hardest things is to maintain our minds at an even keel. Every day, every minute, every hour, it can go off track with the slightest of events that happen every day, or a comment people make that hurts us to the core, even when not intentional. We talk a lot about mental health these days; we talk about resilience, and we talk about mindset. For some, that is easy, and for others, we need strategies to help us along the way.

We all have different strategies that can help. I wanted to share my story of how I went and still go about developing and organising my strategies for myself and my business. The mindset reminds me that I am very grateful that I have managed to create that interest in life, education, and purpose. And, of course, not without the help of ideas/books, systems, strategies, and of course, faith, family, and friends.

My Personal Strategies

Developing the strategies to get out of bed, it was just the start of finding focus and appreciation for my own life and my mindset.

In the process of pulling myself out and taking control, I read a number of books, and I'm not a great reader, so it was bit by bit. They were about positive minds, the leadership of self, and getting along with others, mostly. However, as I said, one was about writing your own life mission statement, another was Tony Robbins, and another was Stephen Covey's *The 7 Habits of Highly Effective People.*

I developed a number of strategies to start every day and be grateful, and to move forward with my own life. Those strategies keep helping me today; sometimes, it's different strategies for different purposes. However, the main point is to create a **clear focus and a positive direction of mindset, believing in yourself and the people around you and being grateful to remain above the line of a positive thought process.**

1. *Make yourself feel good helps your mind feel good.* The first strategies were getting out of bed, having a shower and getting dressed as if I had somewhere to go, making my bed, and having breakfast.

2. *Read positive and uplifting things that are interesting to you.* Not reading the newspaper, but reading something positive and uplifting. This is where Tony Robbins and Stephen Covey come in so much. I had to get away from the negativity of reading the newspaper and watching the news on TV. Now in my monthly journal, I have a positive quote at the beginning of each month and day. Some are my own, some from Tony Robbins or Stephen Covey. Many are about leadership, and Stephen Covey's 7 habits series is never far away. *Being positive and caring helps your mindset see opportunities.*

Leadership is about self first – knowing who you are and how you operate – being the best person you can be, to enable others to be the best they can be.

Slowly but surely, these first two steps helped me become little by little more above the line rather than below it.

I am going to say that it took me at least two years. In that process, I also realised I was very unconfident. I had another friend that took my hand to attend networking events; it took me three months to get up and say my name – nothing else, just my name. It then took me another six months to actually say something decent as an elevator pitch. In later years, I joined Toastmasters, which helped immensely, and now, over the years, I have spoken at events of 250–300 people.

3. *Create a life mission statement.* This is a strategy that guides everything I choose to do in life. Spending the time writing my life mission statement also helped me realise the value of having a business vision, mission, values, and business plan – they guide everything you do in your business. These define a clear pitch that overarches the development of clearly focused strategies.

4. *Become interested in life.* There is so much to learn, see, and do in life, and you don't need a lot of money to do many things. I am creative, so I have lots of interests and loves. I love gardening; I love my family; I love music; I love art, dress designing, sewing – so many things. I love my family, but you have to learn to love yourself, too.

5. *Regular routines create a system.* For me, it has been starting a daily journal notebook. However, your habits can become mind blockers, too, if they are negative. I was brought up in the country 80 miles from the closest town. Out there, you learned to use what you had,

to be creative, and not to waste. With five children living in the same house for 30-plus years, this has also meant in my life I can be a bit of a hoarder. One of my bad habits was being very tactile in my office; in particular, I would have to print things out, and I would write on lots of notes on paper all over the place. And I was not as productive as I wanted to be. Slowly but surely, I have changed (sometimes I slip). However, to change, I again created strategies and habits and focused on that change.

Four Good Rules

A place for everything and everything in its place.

A time for everything and everything in time.

A name for everything and everything to its name.

A use for everything and everything to its use.

These rules are utopian and cannot be kept in their entirety. Keep to them as nearly as you can, and you won't lose by them.

Instead of having lots of paper notes everywhere, I started to buy exercise books. Books for all sorts of things. These days I manage to keep it down to just a couple of books. One for projects and one for my **personal journal.** I have one for each month, which is how I created my daily and monthly journal. It starts with my positive quotes, my mission statement and focus for the month, and a focus on my mindset areas and my to-dos.

My Business Strategies

I started to use what I learned in my personal strategies and adapted them to business to develop very similar strategies and focus for my business mindset.

1. *My own mindset – leadership and self.* **Mastering your own mindset** – focus on positive, open mindset thinking. Be interested in the world.

2. *My vision mindset – planning strategies and goals.* **Dreaming, planning your vision/strategies** – planning continually, trying to encourage others to think outside the square into innovation and creativity.

3. *My relationship mindset – customers and marketing.* **Relating to and valuing people** – creating coaching cultures – helping people to be the best

they can be. Everyone has a value; we have to find that value and work to help them grow their value and ours.

4. *My organisational and systems mindset* **Simplifying and systemising and improving systems** integration and processes. There is just so much in life and business; it's like a spider's web. We don't have to have more so much as to manage simply what we have. For instance, even having a focused plan or strategy helps us to be focused and implement easy - Making life easier.

5. My KPI and financial mindset – budgets, cash flow, pricing. **Performance and profitability** – knowing and controlling the numbers in your business. You can't manage what you don't measure. Know your numbers and measure your targeted results.

My **business journal** also has reminders of what the plan for the month ahead is, the appointments, the to-do list, the phone calls, and the health actions.

Not forgetting, at the end of the day, gratitude for my mindset level and those positive ticks or achievements such as: what I have achieved, who I am grateful for in my life, what I have learned, people I have met for the day, or simply what I have done.

My business mission, purpose, focus, and aim has become:

To encourage, inspire, educate, and support the human spirit. To create and facilitate visions, strategies, and tactics for that competitive advantage through improving knowledge, confidence, performance, and profitability.

Gratitude

Life is never simple; we have lots of twists and turns. In business and in life, I am grateful for those people who have taken my hand over the years. Some are sent to teach us hard lessons, and some just to hold our hands.

It is in the shelter of each other that people live.

– Irish proverb

I am so grateful for my faith. God is always there for me; I just have to listen. I know this by the fact that I have managed to have a passionate, positive, enthusiastic mindset that supports me in realising that there are a lot of people to meet, ideas to have, things to do, and things to see and try in both life and business.

However, realising this, it is important to keep gratitude as a high priority in life. I often write notes and quotes of appreciation to those who have helped me along the way.

Gratitude creates better thinking, better performance, and, in turn, better results.

Mindset: the power of positive thinking – can do attitude, being determined, and taking the hand that reaches out.

Our mindset can break us, or make us get up and dance! It is the most valuable asset that you have next to your spiritual faith, your friends, and your relationships. Our mindset is our driving force, regardless of whether it's good or bad. The power of positive thinking creates the mindset, and results in a 'can do' attitude of determination. A mindset that combines discipline, strength, confidence, and ambition is a powerful one indeed.

Make sure you have a growth mindset, not a fixed mindset. What you think, you become!

Authors

Carolyn's

Gratitude Journal

Available for purchase direct from Carolyn
info@wellnesswarriorsunited.com.au

Dr Carolyn Smith-Keune

Carolyn grew up in remote communities in Papua New Guinea, Northern Queensland and the Northern Territory of Australia. She completed her undergraduate university degree in Marine Biology and Biochemistry in the mid-1990s in Townsville, North Queensland, where she still lives today. She enjoyed a long marine research career, completing both an Honors and PhD studying coral genetics and molecular biology. Carolyn is an experienced author/co-author of numerous scientific papers and enjoyed mentoring many young scientists in the genetics Research Lab she managed for seven years.

In 2018 Carolyn developed chronic daily migraines before finally being diagnosed with complex post-traumatic stress (cPTS), and depression in late 2021. Despite being a busy working mum, Carolyn has turned her life around. Her own adverse childhood and adult experiences have led her to research the neuro-biology of trauma and understand long-term impacts on both DNA (the material of inheritance) and the nervous system (fight-flight-freeze or rest-and-digest responses).

Carolyn is a passionate mental health advocate with her own company, Wellness Warriors United Pty Ltd, developing self-help tools and educational materials for corporations and individuals wishing to address the massive human and financial cost of mental ill-health, and the often-unappreciated effects of intergenerational trauma.

Business Name	Wellness Warriors United Pty Ltd
Facebook	@carolyn.smithkeune
Facebook	@WWUPtyLtd.TRIBE.AUSTRALIA
Linked In	@carolyn-smith-keune
Email	info@wellnesswarriorsunited.com.au
Website	linktr.ee/Wellness_Warriors_United

Helen Cowley's

Business Mastery Journal

Available for purchase direct from Helen
helen.cowley@sbis.com.au

Helen Cowley

Helen has had her fair share of personal battles that step in her path; like many of us, she shares some of her stories and uses her own gratitude and success strategies to develop a mindset of positive determination, passion, and commitment to become a highly experienced and qualified business consultant, coach, trainer, and facilitator. In her 40's, and with five children, Helen started her own business and went back to study, achieving to date an MBA, 2 Graduate Certificates, several Diplomas, and numerous Certificate level qualifications.

Helen has worked for over 25 years with small to medium size businesses and startups. Reviewing and growing their business through planning and supporting their accountability to help them stay on track and improving their personal confidence through implementing simple processes such as gratitude journals.

Helen has been a guest speaker and presenter for radio and TV, Local State and Federal Government, supporting organisations such as Chambers of Commerce, networking groups, and local and state events in Queensland and the Northern Territory.

Helen's mission is *to encourage, inspire, educate, and support the human spirit. To create and facilitate visions, strategies, and tactics for that competitive advantage through improving knowledge, confidence, performance, and profitability.*

Business Name Small Business Improvement Services
Facebook @sbis101
Instagram @sbishelencowley
Linked In @sbishelencowley
Email helen.cowley@sbis.com.au
Website www.sbis.com.au

Jodie's Gratitude Journal

Sunflower Bliss Gratitude Journal

Available for purchase direct from Jodie
sunflowerblissau@gmail.com

Jodie Eustice

My sunflower bliss blooms radiant sunshine, joy and gratitude.
– Jodie Eustice

"Sleep till I'm dead!" is a motto Jodie Eustice has always lived by. But, when life decided to turn the world upside down the last few years, along with her menopausal journey and turning fabulous 50, she was led to finding her soul's purpose and found a sense of wanting a different fulfilment in her life. With that, Sunflower Bliss came from a spiritual deep dive within herself, seeking inner purpose to find her bliss and mindfulness practices.

Currently working full-time in an administration role with the company for over 33 years; her career has had many different roles, with the highlight of travelling to China to implement their product quality system in 2012.

Jodie enjoys travelling with her partner Greg, spending time at home with their two dog's Maisie Mae and Stevie Guinness, a gin & tonic on the back deck and enjoying their garden sanctuary. She loves a workshop and is known to introduce herself as a "professional workshop attendee", as she loves learning various types of arts and crafts and has a passion for creative writing.

Sunflowers are Jodie's joy; they give her a euphoria of blissfulness, sunshine and happiness.

Please connect. I would love to hear from you if the Sunflower Bliss Gratitude Journal and my life chapter story resonate with you.

Instagram   @sunflowerblissau
Email   sunflowerblissau@gmail.com

Kathy's Gratitude Journal

Overcome & Succeed with Gratitude

Available for purchase from
Amazon and
turtlepublishing.com.au

Kathy Shanks

Kathy Shanks is a businesswoman and entrepreneur, as well as a wife of 19 years and a mother of two. She has been self-employed for over twenty-one years as a graphic designer and book publisher.

Not only that, but Kathy is unbelievably passionate about the power of self-development through journaling. She firmly believes that anyone can do anything they set their mind to; all they need is the right tools and beliefs to get them there.

She is the author of *Guided Journaling* and *How to Choose a Side Hustle*, as well as developing over six journaling books and five affirmation books. Through years of her own journaling, she has developed her own process, which she shares in her many books.

Kathy also loves to assist others in becoming self-published authors and journal-creators through her business, *Turtle Publishing*. Self-publishing can be difficult, but with her assistance, clients navigate the self-publishing road, making informed decisions with confidence.

Business Name	Turtle Publishing
Facebook	@kathyshanks
Instagram	@publishing.turtle
Linked In	@Turtle Publishing
Email	info@turtlepublishing.com.au
Website	turtlepublishing.com.au
Bookshop	turtlepublishing.com.au

Michele's

Grieving with Gratitude

Available for purchase direct from Michele
mscotto4@bigpond.net.au

Michele Scott

Michele Scott is the creator of Our Wellness Community (OWC), which is successfully uniting seekers, students, and holistic practitioners everywhere.

Michele is passionate about community, connecting people, and wellness tools & therapies and is giving health and holistic practitioners a voice on Casey Radio 97.7FM via Wellness Conversations Talk Show, also a Podcast on Spotify & a LIVE webcast show on various platforms on Facebook.

Michele has a Diploma of Positive Psychology & Wellbeing, specialising in Positive Coaching and Positive Leadership. She is also an accredited Cappfinity Strengths Profile Facilitator, Holistic Counsellor & Meditation Teacher. Michele has many years of experience in the personal development and wellness field helping her develop an understanding of what drives and motivates people and builds inner peace and lasting happiness.

Business Name Our Wellness Community (OWC)
Facebook @owcvipgroup
Instagram @ourwellnesscommunity
Linked In @michele-scott-coach
Email mscott04@bigpond.net.au
Website ourwellnessschool.org

Nelcia's Gratitude Journal

Living your Best Teacher Life

Available for purchase direct from Nelcia
educatorhealthcoach@gmail.com

Nelcia A. Roehm

Nelcia Roehm (M.Ed.) is an elementary educator and health coach for teachers. She has been in the field of education for the last eighteen years, both in her country of origin, Saint Lucia, and in the United States. Nelcia loves education, but also has a passion for health and wellness. She is a highly motivated individual passionate about children's ministry, health, and wellness and inspires others to live their best lives.

Business Name The Educator Health Coach
Facebook @nelcia.roehm
Instagram @educatorhealthcoach
Linked In @Nelcia Roehm
Email educatorhealthcoach@gmail.com

Patricia's

Manifesting Gratitude Journal

Available for purchase direct from Patricia
patricia@ausinvesta.com.au

Patricia Diano

Patricia Diano is the owner and operator of multiple businesses, is a loving Mother to Massimo, who is ten and Alessandro, who is nine and has a passion for helping and guiding people to remember who they truly are and become the best versions of themselves.

She has spent the past 31 years in the customer lovin' sector across multiple areas in business, including hospitality, hair and beauty and real estate. She has spent the past three years studying and applying her knowledge and expertise as a leadership and mindset specialist.

Patricia is the founder of Silky Nights, a hair care product she designed herself, which protects hair whilst sleeping.

She is the director at AusInvesta Property Advisors and the Senior Property Manager alongside her partner in business and life, Peter, who takes care of the buying and selling.

Patricia also loves the coaching and the wellness space. She has a successful coaching business, specialising in helping business leaders communicate effectively with transparency and trust, increase job satisfaction, build team morale and leverage their strengths in their personal and professional life.

She is also a Bowen therapist as she found the stresses of work and life have a tremendous effect on the body and mind, so Bowen complements the coaching business.

Facebook   @patricia.diano.1
Email   patricia@ausinvesta.com.au

Sharon's

Gratitude Journal

Available for purchase direct from Sharon
info@sharonlefort.com.au

Sharon Le Fort

Sharon is a highly intuitive empath. Whether she is working with individuals or groups, the result is often the same: new perspective, new insights, renewed vigour and changed outlook.

Sharon's background had seen her spending her entire childhood navigating a war zone of domestic abuse, fraught with physical, emotional, and inappropriate sexualised behaviours.

Sharon's determination to believe in herself when no one else did fuels the fire in her belly, becoming a member of a Brisbane-based Domestic Violence Charity's, **Research and Education Committee** and **Advocate**.

Sharon was invited to co-present the *Top 10 Strategies to Rebuilding Your Life after Domestic and Family Violence* and co-chair the lived experience sessions at the *2019 Stop Domestic Violence Conference* as well as co-author and returning author in two of the Charity's Anthology's – *Thriving Survivors Stories from a Lived Experience*.

Sharon went on to create the *Sharon Le Fort – Speaker-Author - Coach*, service. This service empowers women of all backgrounds to gain clarity and purpose in what's next in their lives.

Sharon's mission is to facilitate the healing and guide those who are forgotten survivors of childhood domestic and family abuse and de-stigmatise the impact of childhood domestic and family abuse, mental health and D.I.D.

Facebook	@sharonlefortspeakerauthorcoach
Instagram	@sharonspeakerauthorcoach
LinkedIn	sharonlefort
Email	info@sharonlefort.com.au

Taryn Claire's

Ode to Gratitude Journal

Available for purchase direct from Taryn
tarynclairelenu.com

Taryn Claire Le Nu

As a Breast Cancer Thriver and Survivor I advocate, support, empower, and educate those traversing the tricky terrain of *Cancerland*. Equally.

I used blogging during my cancer journey as a form of therapy to help me process and transition, which culminated in me writing my first book "To Cancer with Love". This book has helped me reach many more women who have been tainted by the Breast Cancer Brush.

Alongside this support to those women, my mission in life is to take people on a journey from spiritual newbies to spiritual know-it-all's. I am passionate about helping people stand in their own power and unlock their true potential. It is incredibly rewarding to be part of this transformative process.

I am an Author and Speaker, a Breast Cancer Survivor and Thriver, I live life with Lymphoedema, I am a Gratitude Junkie, a Rawfood Chef, an Urban Farmer, Beekeeper, Hypnotherapist, Spiritual Mentor, and Shamanic Practitioner.

Starting life doing a Bachelor of Business I gradually expanded into other diverse areas of interest like Raw Food Chef qualifications, Reiki Master, Extended Disc Profiling, Forensic Healing, Hypnotherapy, Timeline Therapy, and Neurolinguistic Programming.

JOIN my Facebook groups: Women Raising Vibration and Le Nu Tribe, I'd love to connect with you there! Scan my code to support my charitable work with women.

Facebook	@lenuhealing
Instagram	@tarynclairelenu
Email	connect@tarynclairelenu.com
Website	tarynclairelenu.com
Website	diaryofadoctorswife.com

Vanessa's

Gratitude Journal

Available for purchase direct from Vanessa
mghealing_4@outlook.com

Vanessa Cirocco

I am Vanessa, and I am an intuitive energy healer. I discovered my life purpose after my spiritual awakening. After healing out of the darkness, I realised I was always living my purpose; now I was just aware of it and opening up to it more. From attracting friends that came from troubled homes or having restrictive parents or attracting partners who were addicts and needed healing. At the time I was so unaware, but after reflection and healing, the signs had been there all along!

After doing a lot of my own personal healing, which I also needed, I've realised my mission is to help people realise their own personal power – how they have the power to change their life and circumstances. I am guided to teaching about how the darkness isn't always a bad place to be, to realise there are lessons to be learnt there. I am an understanding and compassionate healer who holds space for clients when they feel lost or unsure about where they are in life.

I specialise in trauma recovery, mental health, self-love, how to align with your higher self, and for anyone who wants spiritual guidance and clarity for any area of their life. I am a safe space for anyone to come and feel their emotions on a deeper level. Chakra balance healing helps heal energy blocks in your body; I help assist trough the healing and getting to the root cause of the blocks, helping you heal and clear so you can move forward in life, feeling more magical, uplifted, and positive!

Business Name Mystic Goddess Healing
Facebook @mysticgoddesshealing
Instagram @mysticgoddesshealing
Email mghealing_4@outlook.com

www.ingramcontent.com/pod-product-compliance
Lightning Source LLC
Chambersburg PA
CBHW020321010526
44107CB00054B/1930